FOUR-CHARACTER

CHINESE NAMES FOR GIRLS

PART 1

A Collection of Unique 10,000 Chinese Cultural Names Suitable for Babies, Teens, Young, and Adults, the Ultimate Book for Finding the Perfect Names of Girls in Chinese, Understanding Ancient Chinese History & Culture, Simplified Characters, Pinyin, English

一万个中文四字女性名字合集

Duo Duo Wu

吴多多

PREFACE

Welcome to **Chinese Nicknames for Boys** book series. In these books, you will be introduced to **10,000** Chinese nicknames for the boys.

Well, the names are a very important part of Chinese language and culture. Each and every unique Chinese name, made of **pictographic** characters, carries deep meanings as the Chinese names come with huge cultural significances. Chinese parents often spend a considerable amount of time to decide the name of their kids. If you are interested in Chinese language and culture, you are suggested to familiarize yourself with the Chinese names.

In general, the nicknames are made of two characters. The male nicknames generally show the masculine traits, such as bravery, decisive, swift, leadership, etc. The female names show feminine qualities, such as grace, beauty, kindness, etc.

The Han Chinese full names follow the fixed pattern of "**Family name + Given name**". The surname and given name each can be of either one or two characters. Hence, the length of the Chinese names vary from two to four characters. For example, in the name Su Shi (苏轼, Pinyin: Sū Shì, 1037-1101), Su (苏) is the surname and Shi (轼) is the given name. Su Shi is a two-character name. Have you heard this name? Do you know who was Su Shi? Well, Su Shi is the real name of Su Dongpo (苏东坡, Sū Dōngpō), the famous Chinese poet from the Song Dynasty (宋朝, Sòng Cháo, 960-1279). Su Dongpo is a three-character name.

Now that you know these few Chinese characters, you should explore what does Su, Shi, Dong, Po, Song, Chao, etc. mean. All these characters are most frequently used Chinese characters and they are something you must know if you are interested in discovering the Chinese language and culture.

For example, Su is the abbreviation of the name of Jiangsu province (江苏省, Jiāngsū shěng) of China. Hence, every vehicle (car, bus, etc.) registered in the Jiangsu province will get the Su tag on the nameplate (vehicle number). If you say Su Bei (苏北, Sū běi), it means the northern region of Jiangsu province. Similarly, Su Nan (苏南, Sū nán) is the name of the southern region of Jiangsu province. The name of an international airport located in the southern Jiangsu province is Sunan Sufang Airport (苏南硕放国际机场, Sūnánshuò fàng guójì jīchǎng). The airport is located in Wuxi city (无锡市, Wúxī shì), in southern Jiangsu. Further, there is a garden city called Suzhou (苏州, Sūzhōu) in the Jiangsu province. Su can also mean Suzhou. There is a famous university in the Suzhou, the university is called Suzhou University (苏州大学, Sūzhōu dàxué). It is often abbreviated as Su Da (苏大, Sū dà). As another example, the same Su also stands for the USSR, known as Su Lian (苏联, Sūlián) in Chinese. Su Gong (苏共, Sū gòng) means the Soviet Communist Party. Can you feel the depth of just one single character? Just one Chinese character has so many meanings. Next time when you come across a Chinese character, make sure to dig it deeper. It's fun. :)

You can find more resources on my websites (**www.FindChineseNames.com**). There are online tools to predict different types of Chinese names and surnames. You can choose different criteria to generate a variety of combinations of nicknames and names, such as names for boys or girls. You can also find unisex names and nicknames and zodiac for the names based on the year of birth.

www.FindChineseNames.com

-**Duo Duo Wu** (吴多多)

©2023 Duo Duo Wu   All rights reserved.

FOUR-CHARACTER CHINESE NAMES FOR GIRLS

ACKNOWLEDGMENTS

I love Chinese language and culture. Since my Childhood, I have been fascinated by the depth of the ancient Chinese knowledge and wisdom. Finally, I became a Mandarin Chinese language teacher to cherish my dream to spread the ancient wisdom.

It feels wonderful to produce these books to assist the students of Mandarin Chinese learn this ancient language and culture.

I thank my friends, family, students, colleagues, publisher, distributor, and almighty to motivate and support me to author these books.

CONTENTS

CHAPTER 1: Names (1-100)

1	Sha Xun Liangqiu	梁丘莎勋	Liángqiū Shā Xūn	莎 (Shā): Personal and place names	勋 (Xūn): Merit; Meritorious service
2	Ya Lu Duanmu	端木雅六	Duānmù Yǎ Lù	雅 (Yǎ): Refined; elegant; standard; proper	六 (Lù): Used in place names;
3	Han Jing Qiguan	亓官寒静	Qíguān Hán Jìng	寒 (Hán): Cold; Afraid; fearful	静 (Jìng): Still; Calm
4	Ying Yan Huangpu	皇甫颖颜	Huángpǔ Yǐng Yán	颖 (Yǐng): Grain husk; Glume; tip; point	颜 (Yán): Face; Countenance
5	Jing Miao Llvqu	闾丘静苗	Lǘqiū Jìng Miáo	静 (Jìng): Still; Calm	苗 (Miáo): Seedling; Sprout;
6	Yun Ya Yuwen	宇文匀雅	Yǔwén Yún Yǎ	匀 (Yún): Uniform; Even	雅 (Yǎ): Refined; elegant; standard; proper
7	Fen Qiong Ximen	西门芬琼	Xīmén Fēn Qióng	芬 (Fēn): Sweet smell; Fragrance	琼 (Qióng): Fine jade;
8	Ling Wen Dongguo	东郭令雯	Dōngguō Lìng Wén	令 (Lìng): Order; command; decree	雯 (Wén): Cloud in beautiful patterns;
9	Xuan Nai Jiagu	夹谷璇耐	Jiágǔ Xuán Nài	璇 (Xuán): Fine jade;	耐 (Nài): Be able to bear or endure; Tolerance
10	Xin Xi Gongxi	公西新喜	Gōngxī Xīn Xǐ	新 (Xīn): New; fresh; novel; up-to-date	喜 (Xǐ): Be happy; be delighted; Be pleased; be fond of
11	Ying Han Sima	司马盈寒	Sīmǎ Yíng Hán	盈 (Yíng): Be full of; Be filled with	寒 (Hán): Cold; Afraid; fearful
12	Ling Lian Zhuge	诸葛令莲	Zhūgě Lǐng Lián	令 (Lǐng): Ream;	莲 (Lián): Lotus;
13	Bai Lou Shentu	申屠百露	Shēntú Bǎi Lòu	百 (Bǎi): Surname; Hundred	露 (Lòu): Reveal; Show
14	Ling Yang Zhangsun	长孙令扬	Zhǎngsūn Lìng Yáng	令 (Lìng): Order; command; decree	扬 (Yáng): Raise; throw up and

					scatter; Winnow; spread
15	Yin Nai Guliang	穀梁胤奈	Gǔliáng Yìn Nài	胤 (Yìn): Offspring; Posterity	奈 (Nài): But; however; Tackle; deal with; bear stand
16	Feng Zhu Zhangsun	长孙枫珠	Zhǎngsūn Fēng Zhū	枫 (Fēng): Maple; Chinese sweet gum	珠 (Zhū): Bead; Pearl
17	Ying Han Jiagu	夹谷盈寒	Jiágǔ Yíng Hán	盈 (Yíng): Be full of; Be filled with	寒 (Hán): Cold; Afraid; fearful
18	Xuan Zhou Gongxi	公西璇周	Gōngxī Xuán Zhōu	璇 (Xuán): Fine jade;	周 (Zhōu): Circumference; periphery; circuit; week
19	Feng Jing Llvqu	闾丘凤静	Lǘqiū Fèng Jìng	凤 (Fèng): Phoenix; A surname	静 (Jìng): Still; Calm
20	Yue Xian Ziju	子车悦娴	Zǐjū Yuè Xián	悦 (Yuè): Happy; Pleased	娴 (Xián): Refined; Skilled
21	Lian Meng Puyang	濮阳联梦	Púyáng Lián Mèng	联 (Lián): Unite; Join	梦 (Mèng): Dream;
22	Bai Jing Yangshe	羊舌百静	Yángshé Bǎi Jìng	百 (Bǎi): Surname; Hundred	静 (Jìng): Still; Calm
23	Sha Zhuo Helian	赫连沙卓	Hèlián Shà Zhuō	沙 (Shà): Shake;	卓 (Zhuō): Tall and erect; Upright
24	Ning Ning Dongguo	东郭宁宁	Dōngguō Nìng Níng	宁 (Nìng): Rather; Would rather	宁 (Níng): Peaceful; tranquil
25	Sha Wen Zongzheng	宗政莎雯	Zōngzhèng Shā Wén	莎 (Shā): Personal and place names	雯 (Wén): Cloud in beautiful patterns;
26	Xiang Yuan Gongyang	公羊想媛	Gōngyáng Xiǎng Yuán	想 (Xiǎng): Think; like; Guess; suppose; trust	媛 (Yuán): Pretty (used in female names);
27	Yan Xiang Xianyu	鲜于燕想	Xiānyú Yàn Xiǎng	燕 (Yàn): Swallow; Feast	想 (Xiǎng): Think; like; Guess; suppose; trust
28	Ping Sha Ziju	子车萍沙	Zǐjū Píng Shà	萍 (Píng): Duckweed;	沙 (Shà): Shake;

29	Ya Xiao Chanyu	单于雅肖	Chányú Yǎ Xiào	雅 (Yǎ): Refined; elegant; standard; proper	肖 (Xiào): Resemble; Be like
30	Lian Shu Xuanyuan	轩辕联淑	Xuānyuán Lián Shū	联 (Lián): Unite; Join	淑 (Shū): Kind and gentle; Fair
31	Jia ou Ouyang	欧阳伽欧	Ōuyáng Jiā Ōu	伽 (Jiā): Korean musical instrument;	欧 (Ōu): Short for Europe; A surname
32	Yi Xun Dongmen	东门艺勋	Dōngmén Yì Xūn	艺 (Yì): Art; Skill; norm; standard	勋 (Xūn): Merit; Meritorious service
33	Chun Li Xianyu	鲜于淳丽	Xiānyú Chún Lí	淳 (Chún): Pure; Honest	丽 (Lí): Meet with;
34	Yi Su Huangpu	皇甫怡苏	Huángpǔ Yí Sū	怡 (Yí): Happy; Joyful	苏 (Sū): Revive; come to; Short for Suzhou; short for Jiangsu Province;
35	Yan Pin Sikong	司空彦品	Sīkōng Yàn Pǐn	彦 (Yàn): A man of virtue and ability; A surname	品 (Pǐn): Article; product; grade; class
36	Can Qin Puyang	濮阳灿琴	Púyáng Càn Qín	灿 (Càn): Bright; Illuminating	琴 (Qín): Qin, a seven-stringed plucked instrument
37	Chang Xi Tuoba	拓跋畅曦	Tuòbá Chàng Xī	畅 (Chàng): Smooth; unimpeded; Free	曦 (Xī): The sunrise; (Usually of early morning) sunlight
38	Si Ya Gongye	公冶兕雅	Gōngyě Sì Yǎ	兕 (Sì): Female rhinoceros;	雅 (Yǎ): Refined; elegant; standard; proper
39	Zhuo Ge Baili	百里卓歌	Bǎilǐ Zhuō Gē	卓 (Zhuō): Tall and erect; Upright	歌 (Gē): Song; Sing
40	Nuo Nuan Xiahou	夏侯娜暖	Xiàhóu Nuó Nuǎn	娜 (Nuó): Fascinating elegant; Delicate and gentle	暖 (Nuǎn): Warm; Genial
41	Dian Ya Ximen	西门典丫	Xīmén Diǎn Yā	典 (Diǎn): Standard; law;	丫 (Yā): Ah; Bifurcation

				canon	
42	Yan Shi Baili	百里艳诗	Bǎilǐ Yàn Shī	艳 (Yàn): Gorgeous; colorful; Gaudy; amorous	诗 (Shī): Poem; poetry; Verse
43	Si Ning Linghu	令狐兕宁	Lìnghú Sì Nìng	兕 (Sì): Female rhinoceros;	宁 (Nìng): Rather; Would rather
44	Miao Ya Yuwen	宇文苗雅	Yǔwén Miáo Yǎ	苗 (Miáo): Seedling; Sprout;	雅 (Yǎ): Refined; elegant; standard
45	Duo Zhuo Puyang	濮阳多卓	Púyáng Duō Zhuō	多 (Duō): Many; much; more	卓 (Zhuō): Table; Desk
46	Qin Xi Huyan	呼延勤溪	Hūyán Qín Xī	勤 (Qín): Diligent; industrious; Hardworking; often	溪 (Xī): Stream; Brook; rivulet
47	Sha Yi Helian	赫连沙薏	Hèlián Shà Yì	沙 (Shà): Shake;	薏 (Yì): The heart of a lotus seed; Jobs tears
48	Yan Jin Zhongsun	仲孙燕槿	Zhòngsūn Yān Jǐn	燕 (Yān): A surname; North Hebei	槿 (Jǐn): Hibiscus; Rose of Sharon
49	Xuan Ting Xiahou	夏侯旋婷	Xiàhóu Xuán Tíng	旋 (Xuán): Revolve; circle; spin; return; Soon	婷 (Tíng): Graceful;
50	Ze Ting Gongyang	公羊则婷	Gōngyáng Zé Tíng	则 (Zé): Standard; norm; criterion	婷 (Tíng): Graceful;
51	Xin Ling Shangguan	上官昕铃	Shàngguān Xīn Líng	昕 (Xīn): Day; Sunrise	铃 (Líng): Bell; boll; Bud
52	Lu Feng Llvqu	闾丘露枫	Lǘqiū Lù Fēng	露 (Lù): Dew; syrup; fruit juice	枫 (Fēng): Maple; Chinese sweet gum
53	Yi Hui Liangqiu	梁丘怡慧	Liángqiū Yí Huì	怡 (Yí): Happy; Joyful	慧 (Huì): Wisdom; Intelligent
54	Dong Xin Zaifu	宰父冬新	Zǎifǔ Dōng Xīn	冬 (Dōng): Winter; Rub-a-dub	新 (Xīn): New; fresh; novel; up-to-date
55	Yuan Lu Zhongli	钟离媛六	Zhōnglí Yuàn Lù	媛 (Yuàn): Pretty girl; Beautiful women	六 (Lù): Used in place names;
56	Qin Jing	东门勤靖	Dōngmén	勤 (Qín): Diligent;	靖 (Jìng): Peaceful;

	Dongmen		Qín Jìng	industrious; Hardworking; often	Tranquil
57	Miao Jie Ouyang	欧阳淼婕	Ōuyáng Miǎo Jié	淼 (Miǎo): Vast; Wide expanse of water	婕 (Jié): Handsome; Beautiful
58	Xiang Li Baili	百里想丽	Bǎilǐ Xiǎng Lí	想 (Xiǎng): Think; like; Guess; suppose; trust	丽 (Lí): Meet with;
59	Ling Zhu Yuchi	尉迟令珠	Yùchí Líng Zhū	令 (Líng): A surname;	珠 (Zhū): Bead; Pearl
60	Chun Xi Wuma	巫马纯曦	Wūmǎ Chún Xī	纯 (Chún): Pure; Simple	曦 (Xī): The sunrise; (Usually of early morning) sunlight
61	Sha Nai Chanyu	单于沙耐	Chányú Shà Nài	沙 (Shà): Shake;	耐 (Nài): Be able to bear; To endure
62	Nai Duo Yuezheng	乐正奈多	Yuèzhèng Nài Duō	奈 (Nài): But; however; Tackle; deal with; bear stand	多 (Duō): Many; much; more
63	Hui Yi Duanmu	端木慧艺	Duānmù Huì Yì	慧 (Huì): Wisdom; Intelligent	艺 (Yì): Art; Skill; norm; standard
64	Yi Yan Zuoqiu	左丘依艳	Zuǒqiū Yī Yàn	依 (Yī): Depend on; Rely on; comply with; listen to	艳 (Yàn): Gorgeous; colorful; Gaudy; amorous
65	Feng Nuan Zhangsun	长孙枫暖	Zhǎngsūn Fēng Nuǎn	枫 (Fēng): Maple; Chinese sweet gum	暖 (Nuǎn): Warm; Genial
66	Yan Jin Situ	司徒彦槿	Sītú Yàn Jǐn	彦 (Yàn): A man of virtue and ability; A surname	槿 (Jǐn): Hibiscus; Rose of Sharon
67	Sha Ling Guliang	榖梁莎玲	Gǔliáng Shā Líng	莎 (Shā): Personal and place names	玲 (Líng): Sound of jade;
68	Yang ou Duangan	段干扬欧	Duàngān Yáng Ōu	扬 (Yáng): Raise; throw up and scatter; Winnow; spread	欧 (Ōu): Short for Europe; A surname
69	Xiang Yu	东门想语	Dōngmén	想 (Xiǎng): Think;	语 (Yù): Tell; Inform

			Dongmen		Xiǎng Yù	like; Guess; suppose; trust	
70	Sha Ying Duanmu	端木沙滢	Duānmù Shà Yíng	沙 (Shà): Shake;	滢 (Yíng): Crystal-clear;
71	Jiao Yue Taishu	太叔娇月	Tàishū Jiāo Yuè	娇 (Jiāo): Tender; Lovely	月 (Yuè): Moon; Month
72	Jie Yan Dongguo	东郭婕妍	Dōngguō Jié Yán	婕 (Jié): Handsome; Beautiful	妍 (Yán): Beautiful;
73	Wan Wan Yuchi	尉迟婉婉	Yùchí Wǎn Wǎn	婉 (Wǎn): Tactful; polite; Gracious; gentle and agreeable	婉 (Wǎn): Tactful; polite; Gracious; gentle and agreeable
74	Yu Yu Taishu	太叔昱雨	Tàishū Yù Yǔ	昱 (Yù): Sunlight; Sunshine	雨 (Yǔ): Rain; Wet
75	Shi Ling Gongyang	公羊是铃	Gōngyáng Shì Líng	是 (Shì): Yes; correct; right; true; Praise; justify	铃 (Líng): Bell; boll; Bud
76	Chi Dong Zhangsun	长孙驰冬	Zhǎngsūn Chí Dōng	驰 (Chí): Speed	冬 (Dōng): Winter; Rub-a-dub
77	Ning Ying Zhongli	钟离宁瀛	Zhōnglí Nìng Yíng	宁 (Nìng): Rather; Would rather	瀛 (Yíng): Ocean; Sea
78	Ning Zhen Zhuansun	颛孙宁真	Zhuānsūn Nìng Zhēn	宁 (Nìng): Rather; Would rather	真 (Zhēn): Genuine; Real
79	Xian Tong Dongfang	东方娴彤	Dōngfāng Xián Tóng	娴 (Xián): Refined; Skilled	彤 (Tóng): Red; Vermilion
80	Yi Meng Yuwen	宇文忆梦	Yǔwén Yì Mèng	忆 (Yì): Recall; Recollect	梦 (Mèng): Dream;
81	Si Miao Puyang	濮阳兕苗	Púyáng Sì Miáo	兕 (Sì): Female rhinoceros;	苗 (Miáo): Seedling; Sprout;
82	Dai Chun Zuoqiu	左丘代纯	Zuǒqiū Dài Chún	代 (Dài): Take the place of	纯 (Chún): Pure; Simple
83	Feng Ting Zhangdu	仉督枫婷	Zhǎngdū Fēng Tíng	枫 (Fēng): Maple; Chinese sweet gum	婷 (Tíng): Graceful;
84	Xi Sha Ximen	西门曦沙	Xīmén Xī Shà	曦 (Xī): Sunlight (usually of early morning);	沙 (Shà): Shake;

85	Huan Feng Gongye	公冶欢枫	Gōngyě Huān Fēng	欢 (Huān): Joyous; merry; Jubilant	枫 (Fēng): Maple; Chinese sweet gum
86	ai Fang Qidiao	漆雕爱方	Qīdiāo Ài Fāng	爱 (Ài): Love; like; Be fond of	方 (Fāng): Square; involution
87	Hui Ling Diwu	第五慧令	Dìwǔ Huì Lìng	慧 (Huì): Wisdom; Intelligent	令 (Lìng): Order; command; decree
88	Nuo Su Liangqiu	梁丘诺苏	Liángqiū Nuò Sū	诺 (Nuò): Promise; Yes	苏 (Sū): Revive; come to
89	Lan Yi Puyang	濮阳兰怡	Púyáng Lán Yí	兰 (Lán): Orchid; Fragrant thoroughwort	怡 (Yí): Happy; Joyful
90	Xuan Zhan Helian	赫连璇瞻	Hèlián Xuán Zhān	璇 (Xuán): Fine jade;	瞻 (Zhān): Look forward or up;
91	Dian Tao Gongxi	公西典桃	Gōngxī Diǎn Táo	典 (Diǎn): Standard; law; canon	桃 (Táo): Peach; Peach-shaped things
92	Yi Ling Rangsi	壤驷艺铃	Rǎngsì Yì Líng	艺 (Yì): Art; Skill; norm; standard	铃 (Líng): Bell; boll; Bud
93	Qi Bai Gongsun	公孙起百	Gōngsūn Qǐ Bǎi	起 (Qǐ): Rise; get up; Stand up	百 (Bǎi): Surname; Hundred
94	Zi Nai Sima	司马姿耐	Sīmǎ Zī Nài	姿 (Zī): Posture; Looks; appearance	耐 (Nài): Be able to bear; To endure
95	Mei Ling Xianyu	鲜于梅铃	Xiānyú Méi Líng	梅 (Méi): Plum; Prunus mume	铃 (Líng): Bell; boll; Bud
96	Xi Jin Duanmu	端木熙觐	Duānmù Xī Jìn	熙 (Xī): Bright; sunny; prosperous	觐 (Jìn): Present oneself before; Go on a pilgrimage
97	Ruo Duo Zhangdu	仉督若多	Zhǎngdū Ruò Duō	若 (Ruò): Like; seem; As if	多 (Duō): Many; much; more
98	Ting Dai Yangshe	羊舌婷代	Yángshé Tíng Dài	婷 (Tíng): Graceful;	代 (Dài): Take the place of
99	Feng Chi Yuchi	尉迟枫驰	Yùchí Fēng Chí	枫 (Fēng): Maple; Chinese sweet gum	驰 (Chí): Speed; Turn eagerly towards
100	Zhen Yue Situ	司徒真月	Sītú Zhēn Yuè	真 (Zhēn): Genuine; Real	月 (Yuè): Moon; Month

CHAPTER 2: Names (101-200)

101	Wu Ling Qidiao	漆雕伍令	Qīdiāo Wǔ Líng	伍 (Wǔ): Five	令 (Líng): A surname;
102	Jia Lu Sikong	司空伽六	Sīkōng Jiā Lù	伽 (Jiā): Korean musical instrument;	六 (Lù): Used in place names;
103	Sha Tong Baili	百里莎童	Bǎilǐ Shā Tóng	莎 (Shā): Personal and place names	童 (Tóng): Child; young servant; Virgin
104	Zhuo Tan Gongxi	公西卓檀	Gōngxī Zhuō Tán	卓 (Zhuō): Tall and erect; Upright	檀 (Tán): Sandalwood;
105	Xin Miao Wuma	巫马馨苗	Wūmǎ Xīn Miáo	馨 (Xīn): Strong and pervasive fragrance;	苗 (Miáo): Seedling; Sprout;
106	Xi Ying Yuwen	宇文曦莹	Yǔwén Xī Yíng	曦 (Xī): Sunlight (usually of early morning);	莹 (Yíng): Jade-like stone; Lustrous and transparent
107	Si Xi Dongfang	东方兕喜	Dōngfāng Sì Xǐ	兕 (Sì): Female rhinoceros;	喜 (Xǐ): Be happy; be delighted; Be pleased; be fond of
108	Xin Ruo Baili	百里新若	Bǎilǐ Xīn Ruò	新 (Xīn): New; fresh; novel; up-to-date	若 (Ruò): Like; seem; As if
109	Qie Xin Linghu	令狐伽欣	Lìnghú Qié Xīn	伽 (Qié): Temple; Samghrma	欣 (Xīn): Glad; Happy
110	Xin ai Gongxi	公西昕爱	Gōngxī Xīn Ài	昕 (Xīn): Day; Sunrise	爱 (Ài): Love; like; Be fond of; be keen on
111	An Li Yuwen	宇文庵丽	Yǔwén Ān Lí	庵 (Ān): Nunnery; Buddhist convent	丽 (Lí): Meet with;

112	Hua Dian Yuchi	尉迟骅典	Yùchí Huá Diǎn	骅 (Huá): Hualiu; Name of a famous horse	典 (Diǎn): Standard; law; canon
113	Yi Feng Gongyang	公羊懿枫	Gōngyáng Yì Fēng	懿 (Yì): Exemplary; A virtuous woman	枫 (Fēng): Maple; Chinese sweet gum
114	Yue Yu Ximen	西门悦雨	Xīmén Yuè Yǔ	悦 (Yuè): Happy; Pleased	雨 (Yǔ): Rain; Wet
115	Yi Yin Tuoba	拓跋仪寅	Tuòbá Yí Yín	仪 (Yí): Instrument; Meter; bearing	寅 (Yín): Respectful; The third of the twelve Earthly Branches
116	Zhao Lu Qiguan	亓官昭露	Qíguān Zhāo Lù	昭 (Zhāo): Show; Manifest	露 (Lù): Dew; syrup; fruit juice
117	Xin Yan Nangong	南宫昕彦	Nángōng Xīn Yàn	昕 (Xīn): Day; Sunrise	彦 (Yàn): Elegant; accomplished; A man of virtue and ability
118	Bai Ge Gongxi	公西百歌	Gōngxī Bǎi Gē	百 (Bǎi): All; all kinds of; classes	歌 (Gē): Song; Sing
119	Bai Pei Gongxi	公西百培	Gōngxī Bǎi Péi	百 (Bǎi): Surname; Hundred	培 (Péi): Training; cultivate; Earth up; foster
120	Xun Xi Diwu	第五勋喜	Dìwǔ Xūn Xǐ	勋 (Xūn): Merit; Meritorious service	喜 (Xǐ): Be happy; be delighted; Be pleased; be fond of
121	Dai Nuo Sikou	司寇代诺	Sīkòu Dài Nuò	代 (Dài): Take the place of	诺 (Nuò): Promise; Yes
122	Rui Hui Gongyang	公羊瑞慧	Gōngyáng Ruì Huì	瑞 (Ruì): Auspicious; lucky	慧 (Huì): Wisdom; Intelligent
123	Man Wu Nangong	南宫曼吴	Nángōng Màn Wú	曼 (Màn): Graceful; Soft and beautiful	吴 (Wú): Wu, a state in the Zhou Dynasty
124	Yi Yi Wuma	巫马蕙懿	Wūmǎ Yì Yì	蕙 (Yì): The heart of a lotus	懿 (Yì): Exemplary; A virtuous woman

				seed; Jobs tears	
125	Nai Li Yuwen	宇文奈李	Yǔwén Nài Lǐ	奈 (Nài): But; however; Tackle; deal with; bear stand	李 (Lǐ): Plum; A surname
126	Ze Wan Ziju	子车则婉	Zǐjū Zé Wǎn	则 (Zé): Standard; norm; criterion	婉 (Wǎn): Tactful; polite; Gracious; gentle and agreeable
127	Fang Ning Zhangdu	仉督放宁	Zhǎngdū Fàng Níng	放 (Fàng): Release; Set free	宁 (Níng): Peaceful; tranquil
128	An Song Duanmu	端木庵宋	Duānmù Ān Sòng	庵 (Ān): Nunnery; Buddhist convent	宋 (Sòng): Song, a state in the Zhou Dynasty
129	Lian Chun Nangong	南宫莲纯	Nángōng Lián Chún	莲 (Lián): Lotus;	纯 (Chún): Pure; Simple
130	Yue Dian Ziju	子车悦典	Zǐjū Yuè Diǎn	悦 (Yuè): Happy; Pleased	典 (Diǎn): Standard; law; canon
131	Ling Sha Huyan	呼延铃莎	Hūyán Líng Shā	铃 (Líng): Bell; boll; Bud	莎 (Shā): Personal and place names
132	Ning Jing Ziju	子车宁京	Zǐjū Nìng Jīng	宁 (Nìng): Rather; Would rather	京 (Jīng): The capital of a country; Short for Beijing
133	Zhao Zhou Taishu	太叔昭周	Tàishū Zhāo Zhōu	昭 (Zhāo): Show; Manifest	周 (Zhōu): Circumference; periphery; circuit; week
134	Pei Lu Yuwen	宇文培六	Yǔwén Péi Lù	培 (Péi): Training; cultivate; Earth up; foster	六 (Lù): Used in place names;
135	Ling Bai Xianyu	鲜于灵百	Xiānyú Líng Bǎi	灵 (Líng): Quick; clever; Bright; effective	百 (Bǎi): Surname; Hundred

136	Bai Ling Wuma	巫马百令	Wūmǎ Bǎi Lìng	百 (Bǎi): All; all kinds of; classes	令 (Lìng): Order; command; decree
137	ga ou Shentu	申屠伽欧	Shēntú gā Ōu	伽 (gā): Gamma;	欧 (Ōu): Short for Europe; A surname
138	Qin Lian Zhongli	钟离琴莲	Zhōnglí Qín Lián	琴 (Qín): Qin, a seven-stringed plucked instrument	莲 (Lián): Lotus;
139	Zhan ou Nangong	南宫瞻欧	Nángōng Zhān Ōu	瞻 (Zhān): Look forward or up;	欧 (Ōu): Short for Europe; A surname
140	Zhi Xi Wenren	闻人志熙	Wénrén Zhì Xī	志 (Zhì): Aspiration; ambition; Ideal; will	熙 (Xī): Bright; sunny; prosperous
141	Yi Liu Yuwen	宇文艺六	Yǔwén Yì Liù	艺 (Yì): Art; Skill; norm; standard	六 (Liù): Six; 6; number six
142	Song Yin Huangpu	皇甫宋崟	Huángpǔ Sòng Yín	宋 (Sòng): Song, a state in the Zhou Dynasty	崟 (Yín): High and steep;
143	Qing Xi Sikong	司空晴曦	Sīkōng Qíng Xī	晴 (Qíng): Clear; Fine	曦 (Xī): Sunlight (usually of early morning);
144	Yu Lu Sikong	司空语露	Sīkōng Yù Lù	语 (Yù): Tell; Inform	露 (Lù): Dew; syrup; fruit juice
145	Huan Yuan Ximen	西门环媛	Xīmén Huán Yuàn	环 (Huán): Ring; hoop; link; Surround;	媛 (Yuàn): Pretty girl; Beautiful women
146	Yao Rui Chanyu	单于瑶瑞	Chányú Yáo Ruì	瑶 (Yáo): Precious jade; A surname	瑞 (Ruì): Auspicious; lucky
147	Bai Ning Xiahou	夏侯百宁	Xiàhóu Bǎi Níng	百 (Bǎi): Surname; Hundred	宁 (Níng): Peaceful; tranquil
148	Xian Yu Qidiao	漆雕娴蔚	Qīdiāo Xián Yù	娴 (Xián): Refined; Skilled	蔚 (Yù): A surname;
149	Hui Yao	宰父惠瑶	Zǎifǔ Huì	惠 (Huì): Favor;	瑶 (Yáo): Precious

			Zaifu		Yáo	kindness; benefit; Favor; give	jade; A surname
150	Li Fang Zhuansun	颛孙丽放	Zhuānsūn Lì Fàng	丽 (Lì): Beautiful; Pretty	放 (Fàng): Release; Set free
151	Ya Man Moqi	万俟雅曼	Mòqí Yǎ Màn	雅 (Yǎ): Refined; elegant; standard; proper	曼 (Màn): Graceful; Soft and beautiful
152	Zhao Yin Murong	慕容昭胤	Mùróng Zhāo Yìn	昭 (Zhāo): Show; Manifest	胤 (Yìn): Offspring; Posterity
153	Zhi Yue Guliang	穀梁志月	Gǔliáng Zhì Yuè	志 (Zhì): Aspiration; ambition; Ideal; will	月 (Yuè): Moon; Month
154	Ling Tong Yuchi	尉迟令童	Yùchí Lìng Tóng	令 (Lìng): Order; command; decree	童 (Tóng): Child; young servant; Virgin
155	Yue Yue Huangpu	皇甫月悦	Huángpǔ Yuè Yuè	月 (Yuè): Moon; Month	悦 (Yuè): Happy; Pleased
156	Xi Nai Gongyang	公羊熙耐	Gōngyáng Xī Nài	熙 (Xī): Bright; sunny; prosperous	耐 (Nài): Be able to bear or endure; Tolerance
157	Yuan Yin Zuoqiu	左丘媛寅	Zuǒqiū Yuàn Yín	媛 (Yuàn): Pretty girl; Beautiful women	寅 (Yín): Respectful; The third of the twelve Earthly Branches
158	Yin Xing Gongyang	公羊胤幸	Gōngyáng Yìn Xìng	胤 (Yìn): Offspring; Posterity	幸 (Xìng): Good fortune; favor
159	Liu Tian Zhangdu	仉督六甜	Zhǎngdū Liù Tián	六 (Liù): Six; 6; number six	甜 (Tián): Sweetness; Sweet; honeyed
160	Sha Ling Yuwen	宇文沙玲	Yǔwén Shà Líng	沙 (Shà): Shake;	玲 (Líng): Sound of jade;
161	Zhu Huan	漆雕珠环	Qīdiāo Zhū	珠 (Zhū): Bead;	环 (Huán): Ring;

			Qidiao		Huán	Pearl	hoop; link; Surround;
162	Lu Ying Tantai	澹台露盈	Tántái Lù Yíng	露 (Lù): Dew; syrup; fruit juice	盈 (Yíng): Be full of; Be filled with
163	Ting Xi Dongfang	东方婷熙	Dōngfāng Tíng Xī	婷 (Tíng): Graceful;	熙 (Xī): Bright; sunny; prosperous
164	Xi Yu Murong	慕容曦瑜	Mùróng Xī Yú	曦 (Xī): The sunrise; (Usually of early morning) sunlight	瑜 (Yú): Yoga; Fine jade; gem
165	Yin Yu Zhongsun	仲孙胤瑜	Zhòngsūn Yìn Yú	胤 (Yìn): Offspring; Posterity	瑜 (Yú): Yoga; Fine jade; gem
166	Xin Ping Dongguo	东郭昕萍	Dōngguō Xīn Píng	昕 (Xīn): Day; Sunrise	萍 (Píng): Duckweed;
167	Ning Xi Zhuansun	颛孙宁溪	Zhuānsūn Níng Xī	宁 (Níng): Peaceful; tranquil	溪 (Xī): Stream; Brook; rivulet
168	Ge Song Huyan	呼延歌宋	Hūyán Gē Sòng	歌 (Gē): Song; Sing	宋 (Sòng): Song, a state in the Zhou Dynasty
169	Yi Xia Dongfang	东方忆霞	Dōngfāng Yì Xiá	忆 (Yì): Recall; Recollect	霞 (Xiá): Rosy clouds; Morning or evening glow
170	Zhu Huan Xianyu	鲜于珠环	Xiānyú Zhū Huán	珠 (Zhū): Bead; Pearl	环 (Huán): Ring; hoop; link; Surround;
171	Sha Sha Wuma	巫马沙沙	Wūmǎ Shā Shā	沙 (Shā): Sand; granulated; powdered; Hoarse	沙 (Shā): Sand; granulated; powdered; Hoarse
172	Zhan Na Sikong	司空瞻娜	Sīkōng Zhān Nà	瞻 (Zhān): Look forward or up;	娜 (Nà): A word used in feminine names;
173	Xian Dong	闻人娴冬	Wénrén	娴 (Xián):	冬 (Dōng): Winter;

			Wenren		Xián Dōng	Refined; Skilled	Rub-a-dub
174	Qie Xi Zhongli	钟离伽曦	Zhōnglí Qié Xī	伽 (Qié): Temple; Samghrma	曦 (Xī): The sunrise; (Usually of early morning) sunlight
175	Yu ai Jiagu	夹谷愚爱	Jiágǔ Yú Ài	愚 (Yú): I; Make a fool of; fool	爱 (Ài): Love; like; Be fond of; be keen on
176	Yan Xin Zuoqiu	左丘艳馨	Zuǒqiū Yàn Xīn	艳 (Yàn): Gorgeous; colorful; Gaudy; amorous	馨 (Xīn): Strong and pervasive fragrance;
177	Yan Bai Helian	赫连妍百	Hèlián Yán Bǎi	妍 (Yán): Beautiful;	百 (Bǎi): Surname; Hundred
178	Lu ou Sikong	司空六欧	Sīkōng Lù Ōu	六 (Lù): Used in place names;	欧 (Ōu): Short for Europe; A surname
179	Jin Fang Llvqu	闾丘觐方	Lǘqiū Jìn Fāng	觐 (Jìn): Present oneself before; Go on a pilgrimage	方 (Fāng): Square; involution
180	Rui Huan Tuoba	拓跋瑞欢	Tuòbá Ruì Huān	瑞 (Ruì): Auspicious; lucky	欢 (Huān): Joyous; merry; Jubilant; vigorously
181	Hui Ying Helian	赫连惠滢	Hèlián Huì Yíng	惠 (Huì): Favor; kindness; benefit; Favor; give	滢 (Yíng): Crystal-clear;
182	Ning Xiao Shangguan	上官宁肖	Shàngguān Nìng Xiào	宁 (Nìng): Rather; Would rather	肖 (Xiào): Resemble; Be like
183	Yuan Tian Zhangsun	长孙媛甜	Zhǎngsūn Yuàn Tián	媛 (Yuàn): Pretty girl; Beautiful women	甜 (Tián): Sweetness; Sweet; honeyed
184	Yi Fang Tuoba	拓跋意方	Tuòbá Yì Fāng	意 (Yì): Meaning; idea; Wish; desire	方 (Fāng): Square; involution

185	Tian Qing Rangsi	壤驷甜晴	Rǎngsì Tián Qíng	甜 (Tián): Sweetness; Sweet; honeyed	晴 (Qíng): Clear; Fine
186	Yu Zhao Shentu	申屠于昭	Shēntú Yú Zhāo	于 (Yú): Denotes time, location, scope, etc.	昭 (Zhāo): Show; Manifest
187	Yin Lian Gongyang	公羊寅莲	Gōngyáng Yín Lián	寅 (Yín): Respectful; The third of the twelve Earthly Branches	莲 (Lián): Lotus;
188	Shi Xin Yangshe	羊舌是新	Yángshé Shì Xīn	是 (Shì): Yes; correct; right; true; Praise; justify	新 (Xīn): New; fresh; novel; up-to-date
189	Yin Ruo Linghu	令狐胤若	Lìnghú Yìn Ruò	胤 (Yìn): Offspring; Posterity	若 (Ruò): Like; seem; As if
190	Xiao Juan Xuanyuan	轩辕肖娟	Xuānyuán Xiào Juān	肖 (Xiào): Resemble; Be like	娟 (Juān): Graceful; Beautiful
191	Fen Zhi Dongmen	东门芬志	Dōngmén Fēn Zhì	芬 (Fēn): Sweet smell; Fragrance	志 (Zhì): Aspiration; ambition; Ideal; will
192	Rui Ping Zhangsun	长孙瑞萍	Zhǎngsūn Ruì Píng	瑞 (Ruì): Auspicious; lucky	萍 (Píng): Duckweed;
193	Yin Jin Yuchi	尉迟胤觐	Yùchí Yìn Jìn	胤 (Yìn): Offspring; Posterity	觐 (Jìn): Present oneself before; Go on a pilgrimage
194	Na Nuo Situ	司徒娜诺	Sītú Nà Nuò	娜 (Nà): A word used in feminine names;	诺 (Nuò): Promise; Yes
195	Ying Zi Huangpu	皇甫滢姿	Huángpǔ Yíng Zī	滢 (Yíng): Crystal-clear;	姿 (Zī): Posture; Looks; appearance
196	Xuan Ying Tuoba	拓跋旋莹	Tuòbá Xuàn Yíng	旋 (Xuàn): Whirl; turn	莹 (Yíng): Jade-like stone; Lustrous and

				something on a lathe	transparent
197	Fen ou Shentu	申屠芬欧	Shēntú Fēn Ōu	芬 (Fēn): Sweet smell; Fragrance	欧 (Ōu): Short for Europe; A surname
198	Liu Qin Wenren	闻人六勤	Wénrén Liù Qín	六 (Liù): Six; 6; number six	勤 (Qín): Diligent; industrious; Hardworking; often
199	Xuan Nai Llvqu	闾丘璇奈	Lǘqiū Xuán Nài	璇 (Xuán): Fine jade;	奈 (Nài): But; however; Tackle; deal with; bear stand
200	Tao Wu Helian	赫连桃伍	Hèlián Táo Wǔ	桃 (Táo): Peach; Peach-shaped things	伍 (Wǔ): Five

201	Wei Wen Sikou	司寇薇雯	Sīkòu Wēi Wén	薇 (Wēi): Common vetch; Vicia sativa	雯 (Wén): Cloud in beautiful patterns;
202	Bai Sha Zhangdu	仉督百莎	Zhǎngdū Bǎi Shā	百 (Bǎi): Surname; Hundred	莎 (Shā): Personal and place names
203	Yu Ya Diwu	第五语丫	Dìwǔ Yù Yā	语 (Yù): Tell; Inform	丫 (Yā): Ah; Bifurcation
204	Shi Na Zhuansun	颛孙诗娜	Zhuānsūn Shī Nà	诗 (Shī): Poem; poetry; Verse	娜 (Nà): A word used in feminine names;
205	Xin Miao Xianyu	鲜于欣苗	Xiānyú Xīn Miáo	欣 (Xīn): Glad; Happy	苗 (Miáo): Seedling; Sprout;
206	Wan Ying Llvqu	闾丘婉迎	Lǘqiū Wǎn Yíng	婉 (Wǎn): Tactful; polite; Gracious; gentle and agreeable	迎 (Yíng): Welcome; Greet
207	Miao Nai Dongguo	东郭淼耐	Dōngguō Miǎo Nài	淼 (Miǎo): Vast; Wide expanse of water	耐 (Nài): Be able to bear or endure; Tolerance
208	Ying Yu Zongzheng	宗政滢瑜	Zōngzhèng Yíng Yú	滢 (Yíng): Crystal-clear;	瑜 (Yú): Yoga; Fine jade; gem
209	Si Qiong Duanmu	端木兕琼	Duānmù Sì Qióng	兕 (Sì): Female rhinoceros;	琼 (Qióng): Fine jade;
210	Chun Chi Yangshe	羊舌纯驰	Yángshé Chún Chí	纯 (Chún): Pure; Simple	驰 (Chí): Speed; Turn eagerly towards
211	Yin Xue Zhangdu	仉督胤雪	Zhǎngdū Yìn Xuě	胤 (Yìn): Offspring; Posterity	雪 (Xuě): Snow; Wipe out
212	Xi Ze Sima	司马溪则	Sīmǎ Xī Zé	溪 (Xī): Stream; Brook; rivulet	则 (Zé): Standard; norm; criterion
213	Jin Yu Llvqu	闾丘觐蔚	Lǘqiū Jìn Yù	觐 (Jìn): Present oneself before;	蔚 (Yù): A surname;

				Go on a pilgrimage	
214	Jiao Yue Sikou	司寇娇玥	Sīkòu Jiāo Yuè	娇 (Jiāo): Tender; Lovely	玥 (Yuè): A legendary supernatural pearl in ancient China;
215	Dai Yu Zhuansun	颛孙代愚	Zhuānsūn Dài Yú	代 (Dài): Take the place of	愚 (Yú): I; Make a fool of; fool
216	Yi Yan Llvqu	闾丘仪妍	Lǘqiū Yí Yán	仪 (Yí): Instrument; Meter; bearing	妍 (Yán): Beautiful;
217	Ze Zhuo Tantai	澹台则卓	Tántái Zé Zhuō	则 (Zé): Standard; norm; criterion	卓 (Zhuō): Table; Desk
218	Nai Huan Shangguan	上官奈环	Shàngguān Nài Huán	奈 (Nài): But; however; Tackle; deal with; bear stand	环 (Huán): Ring; hoop; link; Surround;
219	Yin Bai Qiguan	亓官崟百	Qíguān Yín Bǎi	崟 (Yín): High and steep;	百 (Bǎi): Surname; Hundred
220	Mei Nuan Qiguan	亓官梅暖	Qíguān Méi Nuǎn	梅 (Méi): Plum; Prunus mume	暖 (Nuǎn): Warm; Genial
221	Ze Yi Llvqu	闾丘则薏	Lǘqiū Zé Yì	则 (Zé): Standard; norm; criterion	薏 (Yì): The heart of a lotus seed; Jobs tears
222	Yu Jiao Chunyu	淳于语娇	Chúnyú Yǔ Jiāo	语 (Yǔ): Language; tongue; Words; set phrase	娇 (Jiāo): Tender; Lovely
223	Shu Xin Wuma	巫马淑昕	Wūmǎ Shū Xīn	淑 (Shū): Kind and gentle; Fair	昕 (Xīn): Day; Sunrise
224	Ya Si Dongmen	东门娅兕	Dōngmén Yà Sì	娅 (Yà): Ya, used in name; Husbands of sisters	兕 (Sì): Female rhinoceros;
225	Dian Pin Helian	赫连典品	Hèlián Diǎn Pǐn	典 (Diǎn): Standard; law; canon	品 (Pǐn): Article; product; grade; class

226	Yan Yi Zhangdu	仉督燕仪	Zhǎngdū Yān Yí	燕 (Yān): A surname; North Hebei	仪 (Yí): Instrument; Meter; bearing
227	Wen Nai Gongliang	公良雯耐	Gōngliáng Wén Nài	雯 (Wén): Cloud in beautiful patterns;	耐 (Nài): Be able to bear or endure; Tolerance
228	Qie Wen Nanmen	南门伽雯	Nánmén Qié Wén	伽 (Qié): Temple; Samghrma	雯 (Wén): Cloud in beautiful patterns;
229	Hua Zhi Nanmen	南门骅芝	Nánmén Huá Zhī	骅 (Huá): Hualiu; Name of a famous horse	芝 (Zhī): A surname; Glossy ganoderma
230	Jin Fang Yuchi	尉迟槿方	Yùchí Jǐn Fāng	槿 (Jǐn): Hibiscus; Rose of Sharon	方 (Fāng): Square; involution
231	Qin Xia Sima	司马勤霞	Sīmǎ Qín Xiá	勤 (Qín): Diligent; industrious; Hardworking; often	霞 (Xiá): Rosy clouds; Morning or evening glow
232	Yan Zhi Chanyu	单于彦志	Chányú Yàn Zhì	彦 (Yàn): Elegant; accomplished; A man of virtue and ability	志 (Zhì): Aspiration; ambition
233	Wan Jing Wuma	巫马曼京	Wūmǎ Wàn Jīng	曼 (Wàn): A surname;	京 (Jīng): The capital of a country; Short for Beijing
234	Yu Yi Sikou	司寇蔚薏	Sīkòu Yù Yì	蔚 (Yù): A surname;	薏 (Yì): The heart of a lotus seed; Jobs tears
235	Hui Yi Zhangsun	长孙惠仪	Zhǎngsūn Huì Yí	惠 (Huì): Favor; kindness; benefit; Favor; give	仪 (Yí): Instrument; Meter; bearing
236	Pei Zhi Gongxi	公西培志	Gōngxī Péi Zhì	培 (Péi): Training; cultivate; Earth up; foster	志 (Zhì): Aspiration; ambition
237	Ying Hua Dongfang	东方迎骅	Dōngfāng Yíng Huá	迎 (Yíng): Welcome; Greet	骅 (Huá): Hualiu; Name of a famous horse

238	Ge Nuo Rangsi	壤驷歌娜	Rǎngsì Gē Nuó	歌 (Gē): Song; Sing	娜 (Nuó): Fascinating elegant; Delicate and gentle
239	Xing Wan Zhongli	钟离幸曼	Zhōnglí Xìng Wàn	幸 (Xìng): Good fortune; favor	曼 (Wàn): A surname;
240	Xiao Lan Baili	百里肖兰	Bǎilǐ Xiāo Lán	肖 (Xiāo): A surname;	兰 (Lán): Orchid; Fragrant thoroughwort
241	Pei Wu Zhongsun	仲孙培伍	Zhòngsūn Péi Wǔ	培 (Péi): Training; cultivate; Earth up; foster	伍 (Wǔ): Five
242	Huan Pei Gongsun	公孙欢培	Gōngsūn Huān Péi	欢 (Huān): Joyous; merry; Jubilant; vigorously	培 (Péi): Training; cultivate; Earth up; foster
243	Jiao Yao Liangqiu	梁丘娇瑶	Liángqiū Jiāo Yáo	娇 (Jiāo): Tender; Lovely	瑶 (Yáo): Precious jade; A surname
244	Wan Dian Liangqiu	梁丘曼典	Liángqiū Wàn Diǎn	曼 (Wàn): A surname;	典 (Diǎn): Standard; law; canon
245	Nai Yang Tuoba	拓跋耐洋	Tuòbá Nài Yáng	耐 (Nài): Be able to bear; To endure	洋 (Yáng): Ocean; silver coin; Vast; multitudinous
246	Duo Tong Ziju	子车多彤	Zǐjū Duō Tóng	多 (Duō): Many; much; more	彤 (Tóng): Red; Vermilion
247	Qin Qi Tantai	澹台勤起	Tántái Qín Qǐ	勤 (Qín): Diligent; industrious; Hardworking; often	起 (Qǐ): Rise; get up; Stand up; draw out
248	Jia Yi Zongzheng	宗政伽仪	Zōngzhèng Jiā Yí	伽 (Jiā): Korean musical instrument;	仪 (Yí): Instrument; Meter; bearing
249	Qing Ying Moqi	万俟晴迎	Mòqí Qíng Yíng	晴 (Qíng): Clear; Fine	迎 (Yíng): Welcome; Greet
250	Yan Yan Zhuge	诸葛妍彦	Zhūgě Yán Yàn	妍 (Yán): Beautiful;	彦 (Yàn): A man of virtue and ability; A surname

251	Xi Nuo Wenren	闻人曦娜	Wénrén Xī Nuó	曦 (Xī): Sunlight (usually of early morning);	娜 (Nuó): Fascinating elegant; Delicate and gentle
252	Zhi Qie Chanyu	单于志伽	Chányú Zhì Qié	志 (Zhì): Aspiration; ambition	伽 (Qié): Temple; Samghrma
253	Tong Meng Shangguan	上官彤梦	Shàngguān Tóng Mèng	彤 (Tóng): Red; Vermilion	梦 (Mèng): Dream;
254	Xiao Liu Duanmu	端木肖六	Duānmù Xiāo Liù	肖 (Xiāo): A surname;	六 (Liù): Six; 6; number six
255	Yi Ling Zaifu	宰父依铃	Zǎifǔ Yī Líng	依 (Yī): Depend on; Rely on; comply with; listen to	铃 (Líng): Bell; boll; Bud
256	ou Ying Wenren	闻人欧莹	Wénrén Ōu Yíng	欧 (Ōu): Short for Europe; A surname	莹 (Yíng): Jade-like stone; Lustrous and transparent
257	Yi Nai Chanyu	单于怡耐	Chányú Yí Nài	怡 (Yí): Happy; Joyful	耐 (Nài): Be able to bear; To endure
258	Li Rui Shangguan	上官丽瑞	Shàngguān Lì Ruì	丽 (Lì): Beautiful; Pretty	瑞 (Ruì): Auspicious; lucky
259	Can Chun Sikong	司空灿纯	Sīkōng Càn Chún	灿 (Càn): Bright; Illuminating	纯 (Chún): Pure; Simple
260	Ying Xing Zaifu	宰父盈幸	Zǎifǔ Yíng Xìng	盈 (Yíng): Be full of; Be filled with	幸 (Xìng): Good fortune; favor
261	Chang Fang Sikou	司寇畅方	Sīkòu Chàng Fāng	畅 (Chàng): Smooth; unimpeded; Free	方 (Fāng): Square; involution
262	Qie Yi Zaifu	宰父伽怡	Zǎifǔ Qié Yí	伽 (Qié): Temple; Samghrma	怡 (Yí): Happy; Joyful
263	Xi Dian Tuoba	拓跋熙典	Tuòbá Xī Diǎn	熙 (Xī): Bright; sunny; prosperous	典 (Diǎn): Standard; law; canon
264	Xun Li Qiguan	亓官勋李	Qíguān Xūn Lǐ	勋 (Xūn): Merit; Meritorious	李 (Lǐ): Plum; A surname

				service	
265	Ying Yuan Guliang	穀梁赢缘	Gǔliáng Yíng Yuán	赢 (Yíng): Win; Beat	缘 (Yuán): Reason; predestined relationship
266	Yi Liu Xiahou	夏侯仪六	Xiàhóu Yí Liù	仪 (Yí): Instrument; Meter; bearing	六 (Liù): Six; 6; number six
267	Miao Tian Dongmen	东门苗甜	Dōngmén Miáo Tián	苗 (Miáo): Seedling; Sprout;	甜 (Tián): Sweetness; Sweet; honeyed
268	Qin Dong Gongliang	公良勤冬	Gōngliáng Qín Dōng	勤 (Qín): Diligent; industrious; Hardworking; often	冬 (Dōng): Winter; Rub-a-dub
269	Feng Zhi Wuma	巫马凤志	Wūmǎ Fèng Zhì	凤 (Fèng): Phoenix; A surname	志 (Zhì): Aspiration; ambition
270	Qin Xi Tuoba	拓跋琴溪	Tuòbá Qín Xī	琴 (Qín): Qin, a seven-stringed plucked instrument	溪 (Xī): Stream; Brook; rivulet
271	Nai Yuan Zongzheng	宗政耐缘	Zōngzhèng Nài Yuán	耐 (Nài): Be able to bear or endure; Tolerance	缘 (Yuán): Reason; predestined relationship
272	Yan Si Huyan	呼延颜兕	Hūyán Yán Sì	颜 (Yán): Face; Countenance	兕 (Sì): Female rhinoceros;
273	Hui Tian Xuanyuan	轩辕慧甜	Xuānyuán Huì Tián	慧 (Huì): Wisdom; Intelligent	甜 (Tián): Sweetness; Sweet; honeyed
274	Ling Hui Guliang	穀梁灵慧	Gǔliáng Líng Huì	灵 (Líng): Quick; clever; Bright; effective	慧 (Huì): Wisdom; Intelligent
275	Ya Yan Zhuge	诸葛娅艳	Zhūgě Yà Yàn	娅 (Yà): Ya, used in name; Husbands of sisters	艳 (Yàn): Gorgeous; colorful; Gaudy; amorous

276	Ya Sha Linghu	令狐娅沙	Lìnghú Yà Shà	娅 (Yà): Ya, used in name; Husbands of sisters	沙 (Shà): Shake;
277	Wan Li Wuma	巫马婉李	Wūmǎ Wǎn Lǐ	婉 (Wǎn): Tactful; polite; Gracious; gentle and agreeable	李 (Lǐ): Plum; A surname
278	Zhuo Lan Zaifu	宰父卓兰	Zǎifǔ Zhuō Lán	卓 (Zhuō): Tall and erect; Upright	兰 (Lán): Orchid; Fragrant thoroughwort
279	An ou Zongzheng	宗政庵欧	Zōngzhèng Ān Ōu	庵 (Ān): Nunnery; Buddhist convent	欧 (Ōu): Short for Europe; A surname
280	Liu Dian Zhongli	钟离六典	Zhōnglí Liù Diǎn	六 (Liù): Six; 6; number six	典 (Diǎn): Standard; law; canon
281	Dong An Guliang	穀梁冬庵	Gǔliáng Dōng Ān	冬 (Dōng): Winter; Rub-a-dub	庵 (Ān): Nunnery; Buddhist convent
282	Can Yu Ximen	西门灿昱	Xīmén Càn Yù	灿 (Càn): Bright; Illuminating	昱 (Yù): Sunlight; Sunshine
283	Bai Yu Jiagu	夹谷百昱	Jiágǔ Bǎi Yù	百 (Bǎi): Surname; Hundred	昱 (Yù): Sunlight; Sunshine
284	Qin Wen Wenren	闻人琴雯	Wénrén Qín Wén	琴 (Qín): Qin, a seven-stringed plucked instrument	雯 (Wén): Cloud in beautiful patterns;
285	Nai Miao Puyang	濮阳奈苗	Púyáng Nài Miáo	奈 (Nài): But; however; Tackle; deal with; bear stand	苗 (Miáo): Seedling; Sprout;
286	Feng Fang Zaifu	宰父枫方	Zǎifǔ Fēng Fāng	枫 (Fēng): Maple; Chinese sweet gum	方 (Fāng): Square; involution
287	Yin Yao Shangguan	上官寅瑶	Shàngguān Yín Yáo	寅 (Yín): Respectful; The third of the	瑶 (Yáo): Precious jade; A surname

				twelve Earthly Branches	
288	Shi Xi Murong	慕容是熙	Mùróng Shì Xī	是 (Shì): Yes; correct; right; true; Praise; justify	熙 (Xī): Bright; sunny; prosperous
289	Wu Yan Taishu	太叔伍艳	Tàishū Wǔ Yàn	伍 (Wǔ): Five	艳 (Yàn): Gorgeous; colorful; Gaudy; amorous
290	Bai Xun Dongfang	东方百勋	Dōngfāng Bǎi Xūn	百 (Bǎi): Surname; Hundred	勋 (Xūn): Merit; Meritorious service
291	Liu Zhao Moqi	万俟六昭	Mòqí Liù Zhāo	六 (Liù): Six; 6; number six	昭 (Zhāo): Show; Manifest
292	Qin ou Gongliang	公良琴欧	Gōngliáng Qín Ōu	琴 (Qín): Qin, a seven-stringed plucked instrument	欧 (Ōu): Short for Europe; A surname
293	Dian Xun Duanmu	端木典勋	Duānmù Diǎn Xūn	典 (Diǎn): Standard; law; canon	勋 (Xūn): Merit; Meritorious service
294	Qin Yun Zhuge	诸葛勤匀	Zhūgě Qín Yún	勤 (Qín): Diligent; industrious; Hardworking; often	匀 (Yún): Uniform; Even
295	Pin Yi Gongyang	公羊品忆	Gōngyáng Pǐn Yì	品 (Pǐn): Article; product; grade; class	忆 (Yì): Recall; Recollect
296	Xin Yuan Gongye	公冶心媛	Gōngyě Xīn Yuán	心 (Xīn): The heart; Mind	媛 (Yuán): Pretty (used in female names);
297	Qi Jing Rangsi	壤驷起泾	Rǎngsì Qǐ Jīng	起 (Qǐ): Rise; get up; Stand up; draw out	泾 (Jīng): Short for the Jinghe River;
298	Duo Yi Tantai	澹台多依	Tántái Duō Yī	多 (Duō): Many; much; more	依 (Yī): Depend on; Rely on; comply with; listen to

299	Ya Yang Rangsi	壤驷雅洋	Rǎngsì Yǎ Yáng	雅 (Yǎ): Refined; elegant; standard; proper	洋 (Yáng): Ocean; silver coin; Vast; multitudinous
300	Xin Yan Huangpu	皇甫心燕	Huángpǔ Xīn Yān	心 (Xīn): The heart; Mind	燕 (Yān): A surname; North Hebei

301	Hua Ning Yuchi	尉迟骅宁	Yùchí Huá Nìng	骅 (Huá): Hualiu; Name of a famous horse	宁 (Nìng): Rather; Would rather
302	Fang Tian Xiahou	夏侯方甜	Xiàhóu Fāng Tián	方 (Fāng): Square; involution	甜 (Tián): Sweetness; Sweet; honeyed
303	Xuan Xuan Nangong	南宫旋旋	Nángōng Xuán Xuán	旋 (Xuán): Revolve; circle; spin; return; Soon	旋 (Xuán): Revolve; circle; spin; return; Soon
304	Yan Yang Huangpu	皇甫燕扬	Huángpǔ Yān Yáng	燕 (Yān): A surname; North Hebei	扬 (Yáng): Raise; throw up and scatter; Winnow; spread
305	Zhou Yu Jiagu	夹谷周语	Jiágǔ Zhōu Yǔ	周 (Zhōu): Circumference; periphery; circuit; week	语 (Yǔ): Language; tongue; Words; set phrase
306	Xiang An Yuezheng	乐正想庵	Yuèzhèng Xiǎng Ān	想 (Xiǎng): Think; like; Guess; suppose; trust	庵 (Ān): Nunnery; Buddhist convent
307	Ou Ling Baili	百里欧灵	Bǎilǐ Ōu Líng	欧 (Ōu): Short for Europe; A surname	灵 (Líng): Quick; clever; Bright; effective
308	Yi Xi Chanyu	单于怡曦	Chányú Yí Xī	怡 (Yí): Happy; Joyful	曦 (Xī): The sunrise; (Usually of early morning) sunlight
309	Zhao Yang Zhongsun	仲孙昭洋	Zhòngsūn Zhāo Yáng	昭 (Zhāo): Show; Manifest	洋 (Yáng): Ocean; silver coin; Vast; multitudinous
310	Nai Shi Yuwen	宇文耐是	Yǔwén Nài Shì	耐 (Nài): Be able to bear or	是 (Shì): Yes; correct; right; true; Praise;

					endure; Tolerance	justify

311	Ze An Sima	司马则庵	Sīmǎ Zé Ān	则 (Zé): Standard; norm; criterion	庵 (Ān): Nunnery; Buddhist convent
312	Yi Jing Gongxi	公西忆静	Gōngxī Yì Jìng	忆 (Yì): Recall; Recollect	静 (Jìng): Still; Calm
313	Xia Yuan Murong	慕容霞嫒	Mùróng Xiá Yuàn	霞 (Xiá): Rosy clouds; Morning or evening glow	嫒 (Yuàn): Pretty girl; Beautiful women
314	Xiao Nai Jiagu	夹谷肖耐	Jiágǔ Xiāo Nài	肖 (Xiāo): A surname;	耐 (Nài): Be able to bear or endure; Tolerance
315	Nai Xuan Wenren	闻人耐璇	Wénrén Nài Xuán	耐 (Nài): Be able to bear; To endure	璇 (Xuán): Fine jade;
316	Man Lan Tantai	澹台曼兰	Tántái Màn Lán	曼 (Màn): Graceful; Soft and beautiful	兰 (Lán): Orchid; Fragrant thoroughwort
317	Lian Zhou Yuchi	尉迟莲周	Yùchí Lián Zhōu	莲 (Lián): Lotus;	周 (Zhōu): Circumference; periphery; circuit; week
318	Yu Tan Yangshe	羊舌瑜檀	Yángshé Yú Tán	瑜 (Yú): Yoga; Fine jade; gem	檀 (Tán): Sandalwood;
319	Bai Jing Huangpu	皇甫百靖	Huángpǔ Bǎi Jìng	百 (Bǎi): All; all kinds of; classes	靖 (Jìng): Peaceful; Tranquil
320	Ge Ling Qidiao	漆雕歌令	Qīdiāo Gē Lìng	歌 (Gē): Song; Sing	令 (Lìng): Order; command; decree
321	Li Feng Tuoba	拓跋莉凤	Tuòbá Lì Fèng	莉 (Lì): Jasmine; Jasmine flower	凤 (Fèng): Phoenix; A surname
322	Xin Sha Shentu	申屠欣沙	Shēntú Xīn Shà	欣 (Xīn): Glad; Happy	沙 (Shà): Shake;
323	Fang Duo Zhongli	钟离方多	Zhōnglí Fāng Duō	方 (Fāng): Square; involution	多 (Duō): Many; much; more

324	Ning Xue Sima	司马宁雪	Sīmǎ Níng Xuě	宁 (Níng): Peaceful; tranquil	雪 (Xuě): Snow; Wipe out
325	Qin Zhou Zuoqiu	左丘琴周	Zuǒqiū Qín Zhōu	琴 (Qín): Qin, a seven-stringed plucked instrument	周 (Zhōu): Circumference; periphery; circuit; week
326	Yu Miao Guliang	榖梁雨淼	Gǔliáng Yǔ Miǎo	雨 (Yǔ): Rain; Wet	淼 (Miǎo): Vast; Wide expanse of water
327	Qing Lian Puyang	濮阳晴联	Púyáng Qíng Lián	晴 (Qíng): Clear; Fine	联 (Lián): Unite; Join
328	Wan Yin Ouyang	欧阳婉胤	Ōuyáng Wǎn Yìn	婉 (Wǎn): Tactful; polite; Gracious; gentle and agreeable	胤 (Yìn): Offspring; Posterity
329	Rui Ling Rangsi	壤驷瑞玲	Rǎngsì Ruì Líng	瑞 (Ruì): Auspicious; lucky	玲 (Líng): Sound of jade;
330	Xin Sha Linghu	令狐昕莎	Lìnghú Xīn Shā	昕 (Xīn): Day; Sunrise	莎 (Shā): Personal and place names
331	Yi Fen Duangan	段干忆芬	Duàngān Yì Fēn	忆 (Yì): Recall; Recollect	芬 (Fēn): Sweet smell; Fragrance
332	Wei Huan Situ	司徒薇环	Sītú Wēi Huán	薇 (Wēi): Common vetch; Vicia sativa	环 (Huán): Ring; hoop; link; Surround;
333	Jing Wu Zhangsun	长孙靖伍	Zhǎngsūn Jìng Wǔ	靖 (Jìng): Peaceful; Tranquil	伍 (Wǔ): Five
334	Shi Xiang Duanmu	端木诗想	Duānmù Shī Xiǎng	诗 (Shī): Poem; poetry; Verse	想 (Xiǎng): Think; like; Guess; suppose; trust
335	Nuo Qin Gongye	公冶娜琴	Gōngyě Nuó Qín	娜 (Nuó): Fascinating elegant; Delicate and	琴 (Qín): Qin, a seven-stringed plucked instrument

				gentle	
336	Can Zhuo Linghu	令狐灿卓	Lìnghú Càn Zhuō	灿 (Càn): Bright; Illuminating	卓 (Zhuō): Table; Desk
337	Jing Duo Yuwen	宇文京多	Yǔwén Jīng Duō	京 (Jīng): The capital of a country; Short for Beijing	多 (Duō): Many; much; more
338	Tong Yu Xuanyuan	轩辕童蔚	Xuānyuán Tóng Yù	童 (Tóng): Child; young servant; Virgin	蔚 (Yù): A surname;
339	Yuan Pei Zhangdu	仉督缘培	Zhǎngdū Yuán Péi	缘 (Yuán): Reason; predestined relationship	培 (Péi): Training; cultivate; Earth up; foster
340	Jing Xue Puyang	濮阳静雪	Púyáng Jìng Xuě	静 (Jìng): Still; Calm	雪 (Xuě): Snow; Wipe out
341	Xian Liu Xuanyuan	轩辕娴六	Xuānyuán Xián Liù	娴 (Xián): Refined; Skilled	六 (Liù): Six; 6; number six
342	Ling Ling Yuchi	尉迟玲令	Yùchí Líng Lǐng	玲 (Líng): Sound of jade;	令 (Lǐng): Ream;
343	Tong Qiong Gongsun	公孙童琼	Gōngsūn Tóng Qióng	童 (Tóng): Child; young servant; Virgin	琼 (Qióng): Fine jade;
344	Fang Yu Duanmu	端木放于	Duānmù Fàng Yú	放 (Fàng): Release; Set free	于 (Yú): Denotes time, location, scope, etc.
345	Ya Nai Duangan	段干雅耐	Duàngān Yǎ Nài	雅 (Yǎ): Refined; elegant; standard	耐 (Nài): Be able to bear; To endure
346	Li Yan Xuanyuan	轩辕莉燕	Xuānyuán Lì Yàn	莉 (Lì): Jasmine; Jasmine flower	燕 (Yàn): Swallow; Feast
347	Miao Han Sikong	司空淼寒	Sīkōng Miǎo Hán	淼 (Miǎo): Vast; Wide expanse of water	寒 (Hán): Cold; Afraid; fearful
348	Yuan Wan Murong	慕容媛婉	Mùróng Yuán Wǎn	媛 (Yuán): Pretty (used in	婉 (Wǎn): Tactful; polite; Gracious;

				female names);	gentle and agreeable
349	Ruo Dai Diwu	第五若代	Dìwǔ Ruò Dài	若 (Ruò): Like; seem; As if	代 (Dài): Take the place of
350	Ge Miao Zhuge	诸葛歌苗	Zhūgě Gē Miáo	歌 (Gē): Song; Sing	苗 (Miáo): Seedling; Sprout;
351	Na Xia Xiahou	夏侯娜霞	Xiàhóu Nà Xiá	娜 (Nà): A word used in feminine names;	霞 (Xiá): Rosy clouds; Morning or evening glow
352	Yu Zhi Yuezheng	乐正于芝	Yuèzhèng Yú Zhī	于 (Yú): Denotes time, location, scope, etc.	芝 (Zhī): A surname; Glossy ganoderma
353	ou Ying Yangshe	羊舌欧迎	Yángshé Ōu Yíng	欧 (Ōu): Short for Europe; A surname	迎 (Yíng): Welcome; Greet
354	ai Juan Helian	赫连爱娟	Hèlián Ài Juān	爱 (Ài): Love; like; Be fond of; be keen on	娟 (Juān): Graceful; Beautiful
355	Duo Dian Shangguan	上官多典	Shàngguān Duō Diǎn	多 (Duō): Many; much; more	典 (Diǎn): Standard; law; canon
356	Yan Xiang Dongmen	东门燕想	Dōngmén Yàn Xiǎng	燕 (Yàn): Swallow; Feast	想 (Xiǎng): Think; like; Guess; suppose; trust
357	Yun Lou Diwu	第五昀露	Dìwǔ Yún Lòu	昀 (Yún): Sunlight; Sunshine	露 (Lòu): Reveal; Show
358	Yao Yin Diwu	第五瑶胤	Dìwǔ Yáo Yìn	瑶 (Yáo): Precious jade; A surname	胤 (Yìn): Offspring; Posterity
359	Yi Yuan Gongxi	公西怡媛	Gōngxī Yí Yuàn	怡 (Yí): Happy; Joyful	媛 (Yuàn): Pretty girl; Beautiful women
360	Tong Xin Qidiao	漆雕彤欣	Qīdiāo Tóng Xīn	彤 (Tóng): Red; Vermilion	欣 (Xīn): Glad; Happy
361	Yun Lian Zhuansun	颛孙昀联	Zhuānsūn Yún Lián	昀 (Yún): Sunlight; Sunshine	联 (Lián): Unite; Join

362	Xi Xi Sikou	司寇溪溪	Sīkòu Xī Xī	溪 (Xī): Stream; Brook; rivulet	溪 (Xī): Stream; Brook; rivulet
363	Jin Zhan Xiahou	夏侯槿瞻	Xiàhóu Jǐn Zhān	槿 (Jǐn): Hibiscus; Rose of Sharon	瞻 (Zhān): Look forward or up;
364	Nuo Yan Zhongsun	仲孙娜颜	Zhòngsūn Nuó Yán	娜 (Nuó): Fascinating elegant; Delicate and gentle	颜 (Yán): Face; Countenance
365	Hui Xi Yangshe	羊舌惠曦	Yángshé Huì Xī	惠 (Huì): Favor; kindness; benefit; Favor; give	曦 (Xī): Sunlight (usually of early morning);
366	Yun Ze Gongye	公冶昀则	Gōngyě Yún Zé	昀 (Yún): Sunlight; Sunshine	则 (Zé): Standard; norm; criterion
367	Yan Zhi Gongliang	公良彦芝	Gōngliáng Yàn Zhī	彦 (Yàn): A man of virtue and ability; A surname	芝 (Zhī): A surname; Glossy ganoderma
368	Chang Yu Moqi	万俟畅蔚	Mòqí Chàng Yù	畅 (Chàng): Smooth; unimpeded; Free	蔚 (Yù): A surname;
369	Yu Ling Zaifu	宰父雨令	Zǎifǔ Yǔ Líng	雨 (Yǔ): Rain; Wet	令 (Líng): A surname;
370	Yang Chun Rangsi	壤驷扬纯	Rǎngsì Yáng Chún	扬 (Yáng): Raise; throw up and scatter; Winnow; spread	纯 (Chún): Pure; Simple
371	Wan Yao Chunyu	淳于婉瑶	Chúnyú Wǎn Yáo	婉 (Wǎn): Tactful; polite; Gracious; gentle and agreeable	瑶 (Yáo): Precious jade; A surname
372	Duo Ting	端木朵婷	Duānmù	朵 (Duǒ):	婷 (Tíng): Graceful;

			Duanmu		Duǒ Tíng	Flower; A surname	
373	Pei Yin Baili	百里培胤	Bǎilǐ Péi Yìn	培 (Péi): Training; cultivate; Earth up; foster	胤 (Yìn): Offspring; Posterity
374	Xia Duo Wenren	闻人霞多	Wénrén Xiá Duō	霞 (Xiá): Rosy clouds; Morning or evening glow	多 (Duō): Many; much; more
375	Lan Yan Llvqu	闾丘兰妍	Lǘqiū Lán Yán	兰 (Lán): Orchid; Fragrant thoroughwort	妍 (Yán): Beautiful;
376	Qi Ling Zhuge	诸葛起令	Zhūgě Qǐ Lǐng	起 (Qǐ): Rise; get up; Stand up; draw out	令 (Lǐng): Ream;
377	Jing Xin Zaifu	宰父泾心	Zǎifǔ Jīng Xīn	泾 (Jīng): Short for the Jinghe River;	心 (Xīn): The heart; Mind
378	Pei Jiao Gongsun	公孙培娇	Gōngsūn Péi Jiāo	培 (Péi): Training; cultivate; Earth up; foster	娇 (Jiāo): Tender; Lovely
379	Jin Yue Liangqiu	梁丘槿玥	Liángqiū Jǐn Yuè	槿 (Jǐn): Hibiscus; Rose of Sharon	玥 (Yuè): A legendary supernatural pearl in ancient China;
380	Lan Yi Linghu	令狐兰仪	Lìnghú Lán Yí	兰 (Lán): Orchid; Fragrant thoroughwort	仪 (Yí): Instrument; Meter; bearing
381	Mei Nuo Yuwen	宇文梅娜	Yǔwén Méi Nuó	梅 (Méi): Plum; Prunus mume	娜 (Nuó): Fascinating elegant; Delicate and gentle
382	Li Qi Llvqu	闾丘莉起	Lǘqiū Lì Qǐ	莉 (Lì): Jasmine; Jasmine flower	起 (Qǐ): Rise; get up; Stand up; draw out
383	Yun Xue Linghu	令狐匀雪	Lìnghú Yún Xuě	匀 (Yún): Uniform; Even	雪 (Xuě): Snow; Wipe out
384	Ya Yan	壤驷雅燕	Rǎngsì Yǎ	雅 (Yǎ): Refined;	燕 (Yān): A surname;

	Rangsi		Yān	elegant; standard; proper	North Hebei
385	Yue Ze Dongmen	东门悦则	Dōngmén Yuè Zé	悦 (Yuè): Happy; Pleased	则 (Zé): Standard; norm; criterion
386	Chun Ping Wuma	巫马纯萍	Wūmǎ Chún Píng	纯 (Chún): Pure; Simple	萍 (Píng): Duckweed;
387	Fang Ping Tuoba	拓跋方萍	Tuòbá Fāng Píng	方 (Fāng): Square; involution	萍 (Píng): Duckweed;
388	Zhi Chi Sikou	司寇志驰	Sīkòu Zhì Chí	志 (Zhì): Aspiration; ambition; Ideal; will	驰 (Chí): Speed; Turn eagerly towards
389	Sha Yan Shentu	申屠沙燕	Shēntú Shà Yān	沙 (Shà): Shake;	燕 (Yān): A surname; North Hebei
390	Yi Yun Jiagu	夹谷意昀	Jiágǔ Yì Yún	意 (Yì): Meaning; idea; Wish; desire	昀 (Yún): Sunlight; Sunshine
391	Tao Xin Yuezheng	乐正桃馨	Yuèzhèng Táo Xīn	桃 (Táo): Peach; Peach-shaped things	馨 (Xīn): Strong and pervasive fragrance;
392	Zhi Nai Dongguo	东郭志耐	Dōngguō Zhì Nài	志 (Zhì): Aspiration; ambition; Ideal; will	耐 (Nài): Be able to bear or endure; Tolerance
393	Jing Yi Sima	司马靖意	Sīmǎ Jìng Yì	靖 (Jìng): Peaceful; Tranquil	意 (Yì): Meaning; idea; Wish; desire
394	Yu Jie Chunyu	淳于瑜婕	Chúnyú Yú Jié	瑜 (Yú): Yoga; Fine jade; gem	婕 (Jié): Handsome; Beautiful
395	Zhen Ying Duanmu	端木真瀛	Duānmù Zhēn Yíng	真 (Zhēn): Genuine; Real	瀛 (Yíng): Ocean; Sea
396	Qiong Hui Shangguan	上官琼惠	Shàngguān Qióng Huì	琼 (Qióng): Fine jade;	惠 (Huì): Favor; kindness; benefit; Favor; give

397	Xi Zhen Zongzheng	宗政曦真	Zōngzhèng Xī Zhēn	曦 (Xī): The sunrise; (Usually of early morning) sunlight	真 (Zhēn): Genuine; Real
398	Yi Chun Chunyu	淳于薏纯	Chúnyú Yì Chún	薏 (Yì): The heart of a lotus seed; Jobs tears	纯 (Chún): Pure; Simple
399	Yun Yun Dongguo	东郭匀匀	Dōngguō Yún Yún	匀 (Yún): Uniform; Even	匀 (Yún): Uniform; Even
400	Ying Ruo Zhongsun	仲孙滢若	Zhòngsūn Yíng Ruò	滢 (Yíng): Crystal-clear;	若 (Ruò): Like; seem; As if

401	Meng Yu Llvqu	闾丘梦语	Lǘqiū Mèng Yù	梦 (Mèng): Dream;	语 (Yù): Tell; Inform
402	Xiang Ying Zhangsun	长孙想颖	Zhǎngsūn Xiǎng Yǐng	想 (Xiǎng): Think; like; Guess; suppose; trust	颖 (Yǐng): Grain husk; Glume; tip; point
403	Ling Nai Nangong	南宫令奈	Nángōng Líng Nài	令 (Líng): A surname;	奈 (Nài): But; however; Tackle; deal with; bear stand
404	Rui Yao Ziju	子车瑞瑶	Zǐjū Ruì Yáo	瑞 (Ruì): Auspicious; lucky	瑶 (Yáo): Precious jade; A surname
405	Yu Li Duanmu	端木愚莉	Duānmù Yú Lì	愚 (Yú): I; Make a fool of; fool	莉 (Lì): Jasmine; Jasmine flower
406	Yu Xin Zhuge	诸葛于馨	Zhūgě Yú Xīn	于 (Yú): Denotes time, location, scope, etc.	馨 (Xīn): Strong and pervasive fragrance;
407	Qin Xuan Gongye	公冶琴旋	Gōngyě Qín Xuán	琴 (Qín): Qin, a seven-stringed plucked instrument	旋 (Xuán): Revolve; circle; spin; return; Soon
408	Ze Ning Chunyu	淳于则宁	Chúnyú Zé Nìng	则 (Zé): Standard; norm; criterion	宁 (Nìng): Rather; Would rather
409	Zhi Hui Huangpu	皇甫志惠	Huángpǔ Zhì Huì	志 (Zhì): Aspiration; ambition	惠 (Huì): Favor; kindness; benefit; Favor; give
410	Ze Lu Yangshe	羊舌则六	Yángshé Zé Lù	则 (Zé): Standard; norm; criterion	六 (Lù): Used in place names;
411	Wen Ling Linghu	令狐雯令	Lìnghú Wén Lǐng	雯 (Wén): Cloud in beautiful patterns;	令 (Lǐng): Ream;
412	Yue Su Tuoba	拓跋悦苏	Tuòbá Yuè Sū	悦 (Yuè): Happy; Pleased	苏 (Sū): Revive; come to; Short for Suzhou; short for Jiangsu Province;

413	Sha Qi Yuezheng	乐正沙起	Yuèzhèng Shā Qǐ	沙 (Shā): Sand; granulated; powdered; Hoarse	起 (Qǐ): Rise; get up; Stand up; draw out
414	Wu Ling Taishu	太叔伍令	Tàishū Wǔ Lǐng	伍 (Wǔ): Five	令 (Lǐng): Ream;
415	Yan Tong Gongliang	公良妍童	Gōngliáng Yán Tóng	妍 (Yán): Beautiful;	童 (Tóng): Child; young servant; Virgin
416	Yu ga Zhangdu	仉督语伽	Zhǎngdū Yù gā	语 (Yù): Tell; Inform	伽 (gā): Gamma;
417	Yu Xing Duangan	段干雨幸	Duàngān Yǔ Xìng	雨 (Yǔ): Rain; Wet	幸 (Xìng): Good fortune; favor
418	Sha Zhen Diwu	第五沙真	Dìwǔ Shā Zhēn	沙 (Shā): Sand; granulated; powdered; Hoarse	真 (Zhēn): Genuine; Real
419	Wei Yue Yuwen	宇文蔚月	Yǔwén Wèi Yuè	蔚 (Wèi): Luxuriant; Grand	月 (Yuè): Moon; Month
420	Yang Lian Chunyu	淳于洋联	Chúnyú Yáng Lián	洋 (Yáng): Ocean; silver coin; Vast; multitudinous	联 (Lián): Unite; Join
421	Meng Yan Wuma	巫马梦彦	Wūmǎ Mèng Yàn	梦 (Mèng): Dream;	彦 (Yàn): A man of virtue and ability; A surname
422	Yun Yu Xianyu	鲜于匀愚	Xiānyú Yún Yú	匀 (Yún): Uniform; Even	愚 (Yú): I; Make a fool of; fool
423	Fen Rui Zaifu	宰父芬瑞	Zǎifǔ Fēn Ruì	芬 (Fēn): Sweet smell; Fragrance	瑞 (Ruì): Auspicious; lucky
424	Qin Yang Sima	司马勤洋	Sīmǎ Qín Yáng	勤 (Qín): Diligent; industrious; Hardworking; often	洋 (Yáng): Ocean; silver coin; Vast; multitudinous
425	Yan Chi Dongmen	东门彦驰	Dōngmén Yàn Chí	彦 (Yàn): Elegant; accomplished; A man of virtue and ability	驰 (Chí): Speed; Turn eagerly towards
426	Xing Qi	段干幸起	Duàngān	幸 (Xìng): Good	起 (Qǐ): Rise; get

	Duangan		Xìng Qǐ	fortune; favor	up; Stand up; draw out
427	Ling Lu Yangshe	羊舌灵露	Yángshé Líng Lù	灵 (Líng): Quick; clever; Bright; effective	露 (Lù): Dew; syrup; fruit juice
428	Sha Miao Gongliang	公良沙淼	Gōngliáng Shà Miǎo	沙 (Shà): Shake;	淼 (Miǎo): Vast; Wide expanse of water
429	Jing Zhu Zhangsun	长孙京珠	Zhǎngsūn Jīng Zhū	京 (Jīng): The capital of a country; Short for Beijing	珠 (Zhū): Bead; Pearl
430	Huan Xia Xuanyuan	轩辕欢霞	Xuānyuán Huān Xiá	欢 (Huān): Joyous; merry; Jubilant; vigorously	霞 (Xiá): Rosy clouds; Morning or evening glow
431	Ying Yi Dongguo	东郭莹懿	Dōngguō Yíng Yì	莹 (Yíng): Jade-like stone; Lustrous and transparent	懿 (Yì): Exemplary; A virtuous woman
432	Ying Wen Huyan	呼延瀛雯	Hūyán Yíng Wén	瀛 (Yíng): Ocean; Sea	雯 (Wén): Cloud in beautiful patterns;
433	Rui Qin Tantai	澹台瑞琴	Tántái Ruì Qín	瑞 (Ruì): Auspicious; lucky	琴 (Qín): Qin, a seven-stringed plucked instrument
434	Jia Rui Zhongli	钟离伽瑞	Zhōnglí Jiā Ruì	伽 (Jiā): Korean musical instrument;	瑞 (Ruì): Auspicious; lucky
435	Wen Li Duangan	段干雯李	Duàngān Wén Lǐ	雯 (Wén): Cloud in beautiful patterns;	李 (Lǐ): Plum; A surname
436	Xiao Yan Yuwen	宇文肖颜	Yǔwén Xiào Yán	肖 (Xiào): Resemble; Be like	颜 (Yán): Face; Countenance
437	Hua Xin Nanmen	南门骅新	Nánmén Huá Xīn	骅 (Huá): Hualiu; Name of a famous horse	新 (Xīn): New; fresh; novel; up-to-date
438	Xi Zhi Zongzheng	宗政曦芝	Zōngzhèng Xī Zhī	曦 (Xī): Sunlight (usually of early morning);	芝 (Zhī): A surname; Glossy ganoderma

439	Nuo Yang Liangqiu	梁丘诺洋	Liángqiū Nuò Yáng	诺 (Nuò): Promise; Yes	洋 (Yáng): Ocean; silver coin; Vast; multitudinous
440	Ling Ying Helian	赫连灵迎	Hèlián Líng Yíng	灵 (Líng): Quick; clever; Bright; effective	迎 (Yíng): Welcome; Greet
441	Xi Ying Tantai	澹台曦迎	Tántái Xī Yíng	曦 (Xī): The sunrise; (Usually of early morning) sunlight	迎 (Yíng): Welcome; Greet
442	Xiao Xing Huyan	呼延肖幸	Hūyán Xiāo Xìng	肖 (Xiāo): A surname;	幸 (Xìng): Good fortune; favor
443	Yao Ze Gongxi	公西瑶则	Gōngxī Yáo Zé	瑶 (Yáo): Precious jade; A surname	则 (Zé): Standard; norm; criterion
444	Xuan Zhan Chunyu	淳于旋瞻	Chúnyú Xuàn Zhān	旋 (Xuàn): Whirl; turn something on a lathe	瞻 (Zhān): Look forward or up;
445	Yin Ying Yangshe	羊舌崟莹	Yángshé Yín Yíng	崟 (Yín): High and steep;	莹 (Yíng): Jade-like stone; Lustrous and transparent
446	Xin Bai Llvqu	闾丘新百	Lǘqiū Xīn Bǎi	新 (Xīn): New; fresh; novel; up-to-date	百 (Bǎi): Surname; Hundred
447	Ping Miao Zhuansun	颛孙萍淼	Zhuānsūn Píng Miǎo	萍 (Píng): Duckweed;	淼 (Miǎo): Vast; Wide expanse of water
448	Zhi Zhen Murong	慕容志真	Mùróng Zhì Zhēn	志 (Zhì): Aspiration; ambition; Ideal; will	真 (Zhēn): Genuine; Real
449	Nuo Yu Gongliang	公良诺于	Gōngliáng Nuò Yú	诺 (Nuò): Promise; Yes	于 (Yú): Denotes time, location, scope, etc.
450	Yao Qing Zhangsun	长孙瑶晴	Zhǎngsūn Yáo Qíng	瑶 (Yáo): Precious jade; A surname	晴 (Qíng): Clear; Fine
451	Feng Zhi	段干凤志	Duàngān	凤 (Fèng): Phoenix;	志 (Zhì): Aspiration;

	Duangan		Fèng Zhì	A surname	ambition; Ideal; will
452	Yuan Yi Gongsun	公孙媛懿	Gōngsūn Yuán Yì	媛 (Yuán): Pretty (used in female names);	懿 (Yì): Exemplary; A virtuous woman
453	Sha Fang Sikou	司寇沙方	Sīkòu Shà Fāng	沙 (Shà): Shake;	方 (Fāng): Square; involution
454	Fang Qiong Situ	司徒方琼	Sītú Fāng Qióng	方 (Fāng): Square; involution	琼 (Qióng): Fine jade;
455	Jing Xuan Gongliang	公良靖旋	Gōngliáng Jìng Xuán	靖 (Jìng): Peaceful; Tranquil	旋 (Xuán): Revolve; circle; spin; return; Soon
456	Ping Qie Helian	赫连萍伽	Hèlián Píng Qié	萍 (Píng): Duckweed;	伽 (Qié): Temple; Samghrma
457	Si Zhi Huangpu	皇甫兕志	Huángpǔ Sì Zhì	兕 (Sì): Female rhinoceros;	志 (Zhì): Aspiration; ambition; Ideal; will
458	Yan Ge Moqi	万俟彦歌	Mòqí Yàn Gē	彦 (Yàn): Elegant; accomplished; A man of virtue and ability	歌 (Gē): Song; Sing
459	Lu Yue Helian	赫连六玥	Hèlián Lù Yuè	六 (Lù): Used in place names;	玥 (Yuè): A legendary supernatural pearl in ancient China;
460	Jin Chun Nangong	南宫觐淳	Nángōng Jìn Chún	觐 (Jìn): Present oneself before; Go on a pilgrimage	淳 (Chún): Pure; Honest
461	Nuo Tan Sikou	司寇娜檀	Sīkòu Nuó Tán	娜 (Nuó): Fascinating elegant; Delicate and gentle	檀 (Tán): Sandalwood;
462	Zhi Tao Yuwen	宇文志桃	Yǔwén Zhì Táo	志 (Zhì): Aspiration; ambition	桃 (Táo): Peach; Peach-shaped things
463	ga Qie Yangshe	羊舌伽伽	Yángshé gā Qié	伽 (gā): Gamma;	伽 (Qié): Temple; Samghrma
464	Yu Fang	百里昱方	Bǎilǐ Yù	昱 (Yù): Sunlight;	方 (Fāng): Square;

	Baili		Fāng	Sunshine	involution
465	Yan Ying Baili	百里燕赢	Bǎilǐ Yàn Yíng	燕 (Yàn): Swallow; Feast	赢 (Yíng): Win; Beat
466	Wen Ning Gongyang	公羊雯宁	Gōngyáng Wén Nìng	雯 (Wén): Cloud in beautiful patterns;	宁 (Nìng): Rather; Would rather
467	Ying Meng Ziju	子车迎梦	Zǐjū Yíng Mèng	迎 (Yíng): Welcome; Greet	梦 (Mèng): Dream;
468	Yan ou Baili	百里燕欧	Bǎilǐ Yàn Ōu	燕 (Yàn): Swallow; Feast	欧 (Ōu): Short for Europe; A surname
469	Zi Shi Murong	慕容姿是	Mùróng Zī Shì	姿 (Zī): Posture; Looks; appearance	是 (Shì): Yes; correct; right; true; Praise; justify
470	Ying Bai Duanmu	端木颖百	Duānmù Yǐng Bǎi	颖 (Yǐng): Grain husk; Glume; tip; point	百 (Bǎi): Surname; Hundred
471	Zhan Tan Gongsun	公孙瞻檀	Gōngsūn Zhān Tán	瞻 (Zhān): Look forward or up;	檀 (Tán): Sandalwood;
472	Jing Yang Huangpu	皇甫泾洋	Huángpǔ Jīng Yáng	泾 (Jīng): Short for the Jinghe River;	洋 (Yáng): Ocean; silver coin; Vast; multitudinous
473	Bai Wei Yuwen	宇文百蔚	Yǔwén Bǎi Wèi	百 (Bǎi): Surname; Hundred	蔚 (Wèi): Luxuriant; Grand
474	Chun Xi Zhongsun	仲孙纯曦	Zhòngsūn Chún Xī	纯 (Chún): Pure; Simple	曦 (Xī): Sunlight (usually of early morning);
475	Fang Yuan Zaifu	宰父放缘	Zǎifǔ Fàng Yuán	放 (Fàng): Release; Set free	缘 (Yuán): Reason; predestined relationship
476	Shi Lu Yuezheng	乐正是露	Yuèzhèng Shì Lù	是 (Shì): Yes; correct; right; true; Praise; justify	露 (Lù): Dew; syrup; fruit juice
477	Zhi Dong Rangsi	壤驷芝冬	Rǎngsì Zhī Dōng	芝 (Zhī): A surname; Glossy ganoderma	冬 (Dōng): Winter; Rub-a-dub
478	Xin Man Ziju	子车新曼	Zǐjū Xīn Màn	新 (Xīn): New; fresh; novel; up-to-	曼 (Màn): Graceful; Soft and beautiful

					date
479	Yi Ping Gongye	公冶仪萍	Gōngyě Yí Píng	仪 (Yí): Instrument; Meter; bearing	萍 (Píng): Duckweed;
480	Li Yi Nanmen	南门丽依	Nánmén Lí Yī	丽 (Lí): Meet with;	依 (Yī): Depend on; Rely on; comply with; listen to
481	Rui Juan Situ	司徒瑞娟	Sītú Ruì Juān	瑞 (Ruì): Auspicious; lucky	娟 (Juān): Graceful; Beautiful
482	Chun Rui Dongfang	东方淳瑞	Dōngfāng Chún Ruì	淳 (Chún): Pure; Honest	瑞 (Ruì): Auspicious; lucky
483	Ling Wu Ouyang	欧阳灵伍	Ōuyáng Líng Wǔ	灵 (Líng): Quick; clever; Bright; effective	伍 (Wǔ): Five
484	Zhuo Yu Sima	司马卓昱	Sīmǎ Zhuō Yù	卓 (Zhuō): Tall and erect; Upright	昱 (Yù): Sunlight; Sunshine
485	Ping Huan Duanmu	端木萍欢	Duānmù Píng Huān	萍 (Píng): Duckweed;	欢 (Huān): Joyous; merry; Jubilant; vigorously
486	Shi Ya Zhuge	诸葛诗雅	Zhūgě Shī Yǎ	诗 (Shī): Poem; poetry; Verse	雅 (Yǎ): Refined; elegant; standard
487	Dian Zhuo Sikong	司空典卓	Sīkōng Diǎn Zhuō	典 (Diǎn): Standard; law; canon	卓 (Zhuō): Table; Desk
488	Yang Yin Moqi	万俟洋胤	Mòqí Yáng Yìn	洋 (Yáng): Ocean; silver coin; Vast; multitudinous	胤 (Yìn): Offspring; Posterity
489	Wei Hua Zuoqiu	左丘薇骅	Zuǒqiū Wēi Huá	薇 (Wēi): Common vetch; Vicia sativa	骅 (Huá): Hualiu; Name of a famous horse
490	Meng Lan Chunyu	淳于梦兰	Chúnyú Mèng Lán	梦 (Mèng): Dream;	兰 (Lán): Orchid; Fragrant thoroughwort
491	Meng Xiao Ziju	子车梦肖	Zǐjū Mèng Xiāo	梦 (Mèng): Dream;	肖 (Xiāo): A surname;
492	Si Tan	公西兕檀	Gōngxī Sì	兕 (Sì): Female	檀 (Tán):

	Gongxi		Tán	rhinoceros;	Sandalwood;
493	Xi Ying Dongmen	东门喜瀛	Dōngmén Xǐ Yíng	喜 (Xǐ): Be happy; be delighted; Be pleased; be fond of	瀛 (Yíng): Ocean; Sea
494	Qing Qiong Dongmen	东门晴琼	Dōngmén Qíng Qióng	晴 (Qíng): Clear; Fine	琼 (Qióng): Fine jade;
495	Xi ou Dongguo	东郭曦欧	Dōngguō Xī Ōu	曦 (Xī): The sunrise; (Usually of early morning) sunlight	欧 (Ōu): Short for Europe; A surname
496	Jing Hui Qidiao	漆雕泾慧	Qīdiāo Jīng Huì	泾 (Jīng): Short for the Jinghe River;	慧 (Huì): Wisdom; Intelligent
497	Ting Shi Zhangdu	仉督婷诗	Zhǎngdū Tíng Shī	婷 (Tíng): Graceful;	诗 (Shī): Poem; poetry; Verse
498	Xuan Nuan Wenren	闻人旋暖	Wénrén Xuàn Nuǎn	旋 (Xuàn): Whirl; turn something on a lathe	暖 (Nuǎn): Warm; Genial
499	Tong Ping Zhongli	钟离彤萍	Zhōnglí Tóng Píng	彤 (Tóng): Red; Vermilion	萍 (Píng): Duckweed;
500	Xuan Yi Linghu	令狐旋意	Lìnghú Xuán Yì	旋 (Xuán): Revolve; circle; spin; return; Soon	意 (Yì): Meaning; idea; Wish; desire

501	Yun Si Puyang	濮阳匀兕	Púyáng Yún Sì	匀 (Yún): Uniform; Even	兕 (Sì): Female rhinoceros;
502	Shi Tong Puyang	濮阳是彤	Púyáng Shì Tóng	是 (Shì): Yes; correct; right; true; Praise; justify	彤 (Tóng): Red; Vermilion
503	Zhao Tao Dongfang	东方昭桃	Dōngfāng Zhāo Táo	昭 (Zhāo): Show; Manifest	桃 (Táo): Peach; Peach-shaped things
504	Ying Zhi Zongzheng	宗政盈芝	Zōngzhèng Yíng Zhī	盈 (Yíng): Be full of; Be filled with	芝 (Zhī): A surname; Glossy ganoderma
505	Jia Ya Linghu	令狐伽丫	Lìnghú Jiā Yā	伽 (Jiā): Korean musical instrument;	丫 (Yā): Ah; Bifurcation
506	Xian Nai Moqi	万俟娴奈	Mòqí Xián Nài	娴 (Xián): Refined; Skilled	奈 (Nài): But; however; Tackle; deal with; bear stand
507	Zhuo Pei Chunyu	淳于卓培	Chúnyú Zhuō Péi	卓 (Zhuō): Table; Desk	培 (Péi): Training; cultivate; Earth up; foster
508	Yun Ying Ziju	子车匀迎	Zǐjū Yún Yíng	匀 (Yún): Uniform; Even	迎 (Yíng): Welcome; Greet
509	Xia Li Gongye	公冶霞李	Gōngyě Xiá Lǐ	霞 (Xiá): Rosy clouds; Morning or evening glow	李 (Lǐ): Plum; A surname
510	Yi Song Sikong	司空懿宋	Sīkōng Yì Sòng	懿 (Yì): Exemplary; A virtuous woman	宋 (Sòng): Song, a state in the Zhou Dynasty
511	ga Xi Zhangsun	长孙伽喜	Zhǎngsūn gā Xǐ	伽 (gā): Gamma;	喜 (Xǐ): Be happy; be delighted; Be pleased; be fond of
512	Jing Shi	西门京是	Xīmén Jīng	京 (Jīng): The capital	是 (Shì): Yes;

		Ximen		Shì	of a country; Short for Beijing	correct; right; true; Praise; justify
513	Jing Li Jiagu	夹谷静丽	Jiágǔ Jìng Lì	静 (Jìng): Still; Calm	丽 (Lì): Beautiful; Pretty
514	Xuan Zhu Rangsi	壤驷璇珠	Rǎngsì Xuán Zhū	璇 (Xuán): Fine jade;	珠 (Zhū): Bead; Pearl
515	Jing Yan Gongye	公冶泾艳	Gōngyě Jīng Yàn	泾 (Jīng): Short for the Jinghe River;	艳 (Yàn): Gorgeous; colorful; Gaudy; amorous
516	Wan Qi Xuanyuan	轩辕婉起	Xuānyuán Wǎn Qǐ	婉 (Wǎn): Tactful; polite; Gracious; gentle and agreeable	起 (Qǐ): Rise; get up; Stand up; draw out
517	Yi Yi Zhongli	钟离薏忆	Zhōnglí Yì Yì	薏 (Yì): The heart of a lotus seed; Jobs tears	忆 (Yì): Recall; Recollect
518	Xi Ya Liangqiu	梁丘熙雅	Liángqiū Xī Yǎ	熙 (Xī): Bright; sunny; prosperous	雅 (Yǎ): Refined; elegant; standard
519	Ying Yi Shentu	申屠瀛薏	Shēntú Yíng Yì	瀛 (Yíng): Ocean; Sea	薏 (Yì): The heart of a lotus seed; Jobs tears
520	Qing Ling Liangqiu	梁丘晴令	Liángqiū Qíng Lìng	晴 (Qíng): Clear; Fine	令 (Lìng): Order; command; decree
521	Ou Pei Rangsi	壤驷欧培	Rǎngsì Ōu Péi	欧 (Ōu): Short for Europe; A surname	培 (Péi): Training; cultivate; Earth up; foster
522	Yi Yi Gongyang	公羊怡忆	Gōngyáng Yí Yì	怡 (Yí): Happy; Joyful	忆 (Yì): Recall; Recollect
523	Xuan Ling Qiguan	亓官旋令	Qíguān Xuán Lǐng	旋 (Xuán): Revolve; circle; spin; return; Soon	令 (Lǐng): Ream;
524	Jing Yuan Chunyu	淳于泾媛	Chúnyú Jīng Yuàn	泾 (Jīng): Short for the Jinghe River;	媛 (Yuàn): Pretty girl; Beautiful women

525	Yuan Jing Huangpu	皇甫媛静	Huángpǔ Yuàn Jìng	媛 (Yuàn): Pretty girl; Beautiful women	静 (Jìng): Still; Calm
526	Xia Chun Baili	百里霞纯	Bǎilǐ Xiá Chún	霞 (Xiá): Rosy clouds; Morning or evening glow	纯 (Chún): Pure; Simple
527	Pei Nai Zhongsun	仲孙培奈	Zhòngsūn Péi Nài	培 (Péi): Training; cultivate; Earth up; foster	奈 (Nài): But; however; Tackle; deal with; bear stand
528	Ya Bai Taishu	太叔丫百	Tàishū Yā Bǎi	丫 (Yā): Ah; Bifurcation	百 (Bǎi): All; all kinds of; classes
529	ai Qing Qiguan	亓官爱晴	Qíguān Ài Qíng	爱 (Ài): Love; like; Be fond of; be keen on	晴 (Qíng): Clear; Fine
530	Xing Xiao Situ	司徒幸肖	Sītú Xìng Xiāo	幸 (Xìng): Good fortune; favor	肖 (Xiāo): A surname;
531	Xiao Nai Zhangdu	仉督肖耐	Zhǎngdū Xiāo Nài	肖 (Xiāo): A surname;	耐 (Nài): Be able to bear; To endure
532	Zhu Meng Dongfang	东方珠梦	Dōngfāng Zhū Mèng	珠 (Zhū): Bead; Pearl	梦 (Mèng): Dream;
533	Hui Zhuo Zhuge	诸葛惠卓	Zhūgě Huì Zhuō	惠 (Huì): Favor; kindness; benefit; Favor; give	卓 (Zhuō): Tall and erect; Upright
534	Zi Shi Qidiao	漆雕姿是	Qīdiāo Zī Shì	姿 (Zī): Posture; Looks; appearance	是 (Shì): Yes; correct; right; true; Praise; justify
535	Bai Li Puyang	濮阳百丽	Púyáng Bǎi Lì	百 (Bǎi): Surname; Hundred	丽 (Lì): Beautiful; Pretty
536	ou Lou Chunyu	淳于欧露	Chúnyú Ōu Lòu	欧 (Ōu): Short for Europe; A surname	露 (Lòu): Reveal; Show
537	Ling Jing Linghu	令狐铃京	Lìnghú Líng Jīng	铃 (Líng): Bell; boll; Bud	京 (Jīng): The capital of a country; Short for

					Beijing
538	Rui Yan Dongguo	东郭瑞颜	Dōngguō Ruì Yán	瑞 (Ruì): Auspicious; lucky	颜 (Yán): Face; Countenance
539	Wu Xi Murong	慕容伍溪	Mùróng Wǔ Xī	伍 (Wǔ): Five	溪 (Xī): Stream; Brook; rivulet
540	Tian Zhu Gongliang	公良甜珠	Gōngliáng Tián Zhū	甜 (Tián): Sweetness; Sweet; honeyed	珠 (Zhū): Bead; Pearl
541	Chun Xi Xuanyuan	轩辕纯溪	Xuānyuán Chún Xī	纯 (Chún): Pure; Simple	溪 (Xī): Stream; Brook; rivulet
542	Feng Chi Ouyang	欧阳凤驰	Ōuyáng Fèng Chí	凤 (Fèng): Phoenix; A surname	驰 (Chí): Speed; Turn eagerly towards
543	Xing Ying Ziju	子车幸颖	Zǐjū Xìng Yǐng	幸 (Xìng): Good fortune; favor	颖 (Yǐng): Grain husk; Glume; tip; point
544	Duo Yue Gongyang	公羊多悦	Gōngyáng Duō Yuè	多 (Duō): Many; much; more	悦 (Yuè): Happy; Pleased
545	Wen Yin Linghu	令狐雯寅	Lìnghú Wén Yín	雯 (Wén): Cloud in beautiful patterns;	寅 (Yín): Respectful; The third of the twelve Earthly Branches
546	Zhuo Yi Linghu	令狐卓懿	Lìnghú Zhuō Yì	卓 (Zhuō): Tall and erect; Upright	懿 (Yì): Exemplary; A virtuous woman
547	Xun Liu Zhangsun	长孙勋六	Zhǎngsūn Xūn Liù	勋 (Xūn): Merit; Meritorious service	六 (Liù): Six; 6; number six
548	Yan Chun Moqi	万俟燕淳	Mòqí Yàn Chún	燕 (Yàn): Swallow; Feast	淳 (Chún): Pure; Honest
549	Fen Nuan Zongzheng	宗政芬暖	Zōngzhèng Fēn Nuǎn	芬 (Fēn): Sweet smell; Fragrance	暖 (Nuǎn): Warm; Genial
550	Chun Tao Ouyang	欧阳淳桃	Ōuyáng Chún Táo	淳 (Chún): Pure; Honest	桃 (Táo): Peach; Peach-shaped things
551	Ling Wei	公冶玲蔚	Gōngyě	玲 (Líng): Sound of	蔚 (Wèi):

			Gongye		Líng Wèi	jade;	Luxuriant; Grand
552	Yan Meng Dongguo	东郭颜梦	Dōngguō Yán Mèng	颜 (Yán): Face; Countenance	梦 (Mèng): Dream;		
553	Yin Ting Tuoba	拓跋崟婷	Tuòbá Yín Tíng	崟 (Yín): High and steep;	婷 (Tíng): Graceful;		
554	Jing Ling Duanmu	端木静灵	Duānmù Jìng Líng	静 (Jìng): Still; Calm	灵 (Líng): Quick; clever; Bright; effective		
555	Xi Ning Zhuge	诸葛喜宁	Zhūgě Xǐ Níng	喜 (Xǐ): Be happy; be delighted; Be pleased; be fond of	宁 (Níng): Peaceful; tranquil		
556	Jin Bai Liangqiu	梁丘觐百	Liángqiū Jìn Bǎi	觐 (Jìn): Present oneself before; Go on a pilgrimage	百 (Bǎi): All; all kinds of; classes		
557	Tong Miao Gongye	公冶童淼	Gōngyě Tóng Miǎo	童 (Tóng): Child; young servant; Virgin	淼 (Miǎo): Vast; Wide expanse of water		
558	Li Hua Zhongli	钟离莉骅	Zhōnglí Lì Huá	莉 (Lì): Jasmine; Jasmine flower	骅 (Huá): Hualiu; Name of a famous horse		
559	Liu Jin Shentu	申屠六槿	Shēntú Liù Jǐn	六 (Liù): Six; 6; number six	槿 (Jǐn): Hibiscus; Rose of Sharon		
560	Qie Jing Gongliang	公良伽泾	Gōngliáng Qié Jīng	伽 (Qié): Temple; Samghrma	泾 (Jīng): Short for the Jinghe River;		
561	Xin Jin Baili	百里欣觐	Bǎilǐ Xīn Jìn	欣 (Xīn): Glad; Happy	觐 (Jìn): Present oneself before; Go on a pilgrimage		
562	Fen Xi Shentu	申屠芬曦	Shēntú Fēn Xī	芬 (Fēn): Sweet smell; Fragrance	曦 (Xī): The sunrise; (Usually of early morning) sunlight		
563	Lian Dong Wenren	闻人联冬	Wénrén Lián Dōng	联 (Lián): Unite; Join	冬 (Dōng): Winter; Rub-a-dub		

564	Yin Yan Sikong	司空寅颜	Sīkōng Yín Yán	寅 (Yín): Respectful; The third of the twelve Earthly Branches	颜 (Yán): Face; Countenance
565	Zhen An Taishu	太叔真庵	Tàishū Zhēn Ān	真 (Zhēn): Genuine; Real	庵 (Ān): Nunnery; Buddhist convent
566	Wei Huan Liangqiu	梁丘薇环	Liángqiū Wēi Huán	薇 (Wēi): Common vetch; Vicia sativa	环 (Huán): Ring; hoop; link; Surround;
567	Ning Wei Zhuge	诸葛宁蔚	Zhūgě Níng Wèi	宁 (Níng): Peaceful; tranquil	蔚 (Wèi): Luxuriant; Grand
568	Ying Qie Dongmen	东门滢伽	Dōngmén Yíng Qié	滢 (Yíng): Crystal-clear;	伽 (Qié): Temple; Samghrma
569	Xi Ying Chanyu	单于溪莹	Chányú Xī Yíng	溪 (Xī): Stream; Brook; rivulet	莹 (Yíng): Jade-like stone; Lustrous and transparent
570	Nai Xin Zhangsun	长孙奈新	Zhǎngsūn Nài Xīn	奈 (Nài): But; however; Tackle; deal with; bear stand	新 (Xīn): New; fresh; novel; up-to-date
571	Ying Ya Qidiao	漆雕莹娅	Qīdiāo Yíng Yà	莹 (Yíng): Jade-like stone; Lustrous and transparent	娅 (Yà): Ya, used in name; Husbands of sisters
572	Yi Rui Helian	赫连忆瑞	Hèlián Yì Ruì	忆 (Yì): Recall; Recollect	瑞 (Ruì): Auspicious; lucky
573	Chun Zhuo Yuchi	尉迟淳卓	Yùchí Chún Zhuō	淳 (Chún): Pure; Honest	卓 (Zhuō): Tall and erect; Upright
574	Duo Jing Liangqiu	梁丘朵泾	Liángqiū Duǒ Jīng	朵 (Duǒ): Flower; A surname	泾 (Jīng): Short for the Jinghe River;
575	Ling Ruo Ouyang	欧阳令若	Ōuyáng Lìng Ruò	令 (Lìng): Order; command; decree	若 (Ruò): Like; seem; As if
576	Xi Fen Xuanyuan	轩辕曦芬	Xuānyuán Xī Fēn	曦 (Xī): The sunrise; (Usually of early	芬 (Fēn): Sweet smell; Fragrance

				morning) sunlight	
577	Yu Zhen Sikong	司空愚真	Sīkōng Yú Zhēn	愚 (Yú): I; Make a fool of; fool	真 (Zhēn): Genuine; Real
578	Yu Zhu Shentu	申屠语珠	Shēntú Yǔ Zhū	语 (Yǔ): Language; tongue; Words; set phrase	珠 (Zhū): Bead; Pearl
579	Xin Ying Xiahou	夏侯馨滢	Xiàhóu Xīn Yíng	馨 (Xīn): Strong and pervasive fragrance;	滢 (Yíng): Crystal-clear;
580	Yun Song Taishu	太叔昀宋	Tàishū Yún Sòng	昀 (Yún): Sunlight; Sunshine	宋 (Sòng): Song, a state in the Zhou Dynasty
581	Xiao Nai Diwu	第五肖奈	Dìwǔ Xiào Nài	肖 (Xiào): Resemble; Be like	奈 (Nài): But; however; Tackle; deal with; bear stand
582	Yi Na Gongyang	公羊艺娜	Gōngyáng Yì Nà	艺 (Yì): Art; Skill; norm; standard	娜 (Nà): A word used in feminine names;
583	Miao Chun Yuwen	宇文苗纯	Yǔwén Miáo Chún	苗 (Miáo): Seedling; Sprout;	纯 (Chún): Pure; Simple
584	Mei Yi Duangan	段干梅意	Duàngān Méi Yì	梅 (Méi): Plum; Prunus mume	意 (Yì): Meaning; idea; Wish; desire
585	Jia Ya Ziju	子车伽雅	Zǐjū Jiā Yǎ	伽 (Jiā): Korean musical instrument;	雅 (Yǎ): Refined; elegant; standard
586	Yan Lian Yuwen	宇文妍联	Yǔwén Yán Lián	妍 (Yán): Beautiful;	联 (Lián): Unite; Join
587	Ling Xiao Dongmen	东门令肖	Dōngmén Líng Xiāo	令 (Líng): A surname;	肖 (Xiāo): A surname;
588	Yang Mei Gongyang	公羊洋梅	Gōngyáng Yáng Méi	洋 (Yáng): Ocean; silver coin; Vast; multitudinous	梅 (Méi): Plum; Prunus mume
589	Tan Yi Diwu	第五檀薏	Dìwǔ Tán Yì	檀 (Tán): Sandalwood;	薏 (Yì): The heart of a lotus seed; Jobs tears
590	Ying Xuan	漆雕颖旋	Qīdiāo	颖 (Yǐng): Grain	旋 (Xuán):

			Yǐng Xuán	husk; Glume; tip; point	Revolve; circle; spin; return; Soon
	Qidiao				
591	Xia Jie Xianyu	鲜于霞婕	Xiānyú Xiá Jié	霞 (Xiá): Rosy clouds; Morning or evening glow	婕 (Jié): Handsome; Beautiful
592	Fang Yang Rangsi	壤驷方洋	Rǎngsì Fāng Yáng	方 (Fāng): Square; involution	洋 (Yáng): Ocean; silver coin; Vast; multitudinous
593	Xiao Ying Diwu	第五肖颖	Dìwǔ Xiào Yǐng	肖 (Xiào): Resemble; Be like	颖 (Yǐng): Grain husk; Glume; tip; point
594	ou Feng Ximen	西门欧凤	Xīmén Ōu Fèng	欧 (Ōu): Short for Europe; A surname	凤 (Fèng): Phoenix; A surname
595	Yi Xi Taishu	太叔仪溪	Tàishū Yí Xī	仪 (Yí): Instrument; Meter; bearing	溪 (Xī): Stream; Brook; rivulet
596	ou Ge Liangqiu	梁丘欧歌	Liángqiū Ōu Gē	欧 (Ōu): Short for Europe; A surname	歌 (Gē): Song; Sing
597	Yu Zhen Qiguan	亓官昱真	Qíguān Yù Zhēn	昱 (Yù): Sunlight; Sunshine	真 (Zhēn): Genuine; Real
598	Yu Zhuo Duangan	段干于卓	Duàngān Yú Zhuō	于 (Yú): Denotes time, location, scope, etc.	卓 (Zhuō): Table; Desk
599	Duo Hui Puyang	濮阳朵慧	Púyáng Duǒ Huì	朵 (Duǒ): Flower; A surname	慧 (Huì): Wisdom; Intelligent
600	Yu Yin Yuchi	尉迟瑜崟	Yùchí Yú Yín	瑜 (Yú): Yoga; Fine jade; gem	崟 (Yín): High and steep;

601	Zi Zhi Gongyang	公羊姿志	Gōngyáng Zī Zhì	姿 (Zī): Posture; Looks; appearance	志 (Zhì): Aspiration; ambition; Ideal; will
602	Nuo Xuan Xianyu	鲜于诺旋	Xiānyú Nuò Xuán	诺 (Nuò): Promise; Yes	旋 (Xuán): Revolve; circle; spin; return; Soon
603	Pei Xuan Nangong	南宫培旋	Nángōng Péi Xuàn	培 (Péi): Training; cultivate; Earth up; foster	旋 (Xuàn): Whirl; turn something on a lathe
604	Yu Yi Zhuansun	颛孙蔚懿	Zhuānsūn Yù Yì	蔚 (Yù): A surname;	懿 (Yì): Exemplary; A virtuous woman
605	Yu Wan Guliang	穀梁语曼	Gǔliáng Yù Wàn	语 (Yù): Tell; Inform	曼 (Wàn): A surname;
606	Li Shi Yangshe	羊舌莉是	Yángshé Lì Shì	莉 (Lì): Jasmine; Jasmine flower	是 (Shì): Yes; correct; right; true; Praise; justify
607	Yi Ling Ziju	子车怡铃	Zǐjū Yí Líng	怡 (Yí): Happy; Joyful	铃 (Líng): Bell; boll; Bud
608	Bai Yuan Xuanyuan	轩辕百缘	Xuānyuán Bǎi Yuán	百 (Bǎi): All; all kinds of; classes	缘 (Yuán): Reason; predestined relationship
609	Jing Ge Qiguan	亓官靖歌	Qíguān Jìng Gē	靖 (Jìng): Peaceful; Tranquil	歌 (Gē): Song; Sing
610	Yan Duo Xiahou	夏侯彦多	Xiàhóu Yàn Duō	彦 (Yàn): A man of virtue and ability; A surname	多 (Duō): Many; much; more
611	Lu Li Murong	慕容六丽	Mùróng Lù Lì	六 (Lù): Used in place names;	丽 (Lì): Beautiful; Pretty
612	Ya Ya Wuma	巫马雅丫	Wūmǎ Yǎ Yā	雅 (Yǎ): Refined; elegant; standard; proper	丫 (Yā): Ah; Bifurcation
613	Dai Xi	澹台代曦	Tántái Dài	代 (Dài): Take the	曦 (Xī): Sunlight

			Tantai		Xī	place of	(usually of early morning);
614	Xun Chun Moqi	万俟勋纯	Mòqí Xūn Chún	勋 (Xūn): Merit; Meritorious service	纯 (Chún): Pure; Simple
615	Xiang Yu Zaifu	宰父想昱	Zǎifǔ Xiǎng Yù	想 (Xiǎng): Think; like; Guess; suppose; trust	昱 (Yù): Sunlight; Sunshine
616	Yu Yi Shangguan	上官昱仪	Shàngguān Yù Yí	昱 (Yù): Sunlight; Sunshine	仪 (Yí): Instrument; Meter; bearing
617	Liu Yuan Ziju	子车六媛	Zǐjū Liù Yuàn	六 (Liù): Six; 6; number six	媛 (Yuàn): Pretty girl; Beautiful women
618	Wei Ying Nanmen	南门蔚颖	Nánmén Wèi Yǐng	蔚 (Wèi): Luxuriant; Grand	颖 (Yǐng): Grain husk; Glume; tip; point
619	Feng Wan Gongye	公冶枫婉	Gōngyě Fēng Wǎn	枫 (Fēng): Maple; Chinese sweet gum	婉 (Wǎn): Tactful; polite; Gracious; gentle and agreeable
620	Ge Hui Jiagu	夹谷歌惠	Jiágǔ Gē Huì	歌 (Gē): Song; Sing	惠 (Huì): Favor; kindness; benefit; Favor; give
621	Man Ya Wuma	巫马曼雅	Wūmǎ Màn Yǎ	曼 (Màn): Graceful; Soft and beautiful	雅 (Yǎ): Refined; elegant; standard; proper
622	Zhou Miao Rangsi	壤驷周淼	Rǎngsì Zhōu Miǎo	周 (Zhōu): Circumference; periphery; circuit; week	淼 (Miǎo): Vast; Wide expanse of water
623	Yu Xin Yangshe	羊舌昱新	Yángshé Yù Xīn	昱 (Yù): Sunlight; Sunshine	新 (Xīn): New; fresh; novel; up-to-date
624	Pei ai Wuma	巫马培爱	Wūmǎ Péi Ài	培 (Péi): Training; cultivate; Earth up;	爱 (Ài): Love; like; Be fond of; be

				foster	keen on
625	Zhi Nuo Duangan	段干志娜	Duàngān Zhì Nuó	志 (Zhì): Aspiration; ambition	娜 (Nuó): Fascinating elegant; Delicate and gentle
626	Chi Jie Dongfang	东方驰婕	Dōngfāng Chí Jié	驰 (Chí): Speed; Turn eagerly towards	婕 (Jié): Handsome; Beautiful
627	Jing Dong Zhuansun	颛孙京冬	Zhuānsūn Jīng Dōng	京 (Jīng): The capital of a country; Short for Beijing	冬 (Dōng): Winter; Rub-a-dub
628	Xuan Sha Yangshe	羊舌旋沙	Yángshé Xuàn Shà	旋 (Xuàn): Whirl; turn something on a lathe	沙 (Shà): Shake;
629	Hui Qing Tantai	澹台慧晴	Tántái Huì Qíng	慧 (Huì): Wisdom; Intelligent	晴 (Qíng): Clear; Fine
630	Jing Yue Dongfang	东方靖月	Dōngfāng Jìng Yuè	靖 (Jìng): Peaceful; Tranquil	月 (Yuè): Moon; Month
631	Yi Chang Shangguan	上官薏畅	Shàngguān Yì Chàng	薏 (Yì): The heart of a lotus seed; Jobs tears	畅 (Chàng): Smooth; unimpeded; Free
632	Chi Qin Chunyu	淳于驰勤	Chúnyú Chí Qín	驰 (Chí): Speed; Turn eagerly towards	勤 (Qín): Diligent; industrious; Hardworking; often
633	Tian Xi Liangqiu	梁丘甜熙	Liángqiū Tián Xī	甜 (Tián): Sweetness; Sweet; honeyed	熙 (Xī): Bright; sunny; prosperous
634	Ying Xiao Gongyang	公羊迎肖	Gōngyáng Yíng Xiào	迎 (Yíng): Welcome; Greet	肖 (Xiào): Resemble; Be like
635	Hui Wu Yuwen	宇文惠吴	Yǔwén Huì Wú	惠 (Huì): Favor; kindness; benefit; Favor; give	吴 (Wú): Wu, a state in the Zhou Dynasty
636	Sha Nai Duanmu	端木莎耐	Duānmù Shā Nài	莎 (Shā): Personal and place names	耐 (Nài): Be able to bear or endure;

				Tolerance
637	Ruo Lou Xiahou	夏侯若露	Xiàhóu Ruò Lòu	若 (Ruò): Like; seem; As if	露 (Lòu): Reveal; Show
638	Mei Nai Jiagu	夹谷梅耐	Jiágǔ Méi Nài	梅 (Méi): Plum; Prunus mume	耐 (Nài): Be able to bear or endure; Tolerance
639	Ping Xi Huangpu	皇甫萍曦	Huángpǔ Píng Xī	萍 (Píng): Duckweed;	曦 (Xī): Sunlight (usually of early morning);
640	Yan Ping Zuoqiu	左丘燕萍	Zuǒqiū Yān Píng	燕 (Yān): A surname; North Hebei	萍 (Píng): Duckweed;
641	Qi Xi Zhangdu	仉督起溪	Zhǎngdū Qǐ Xī	起 (Qǐ): Rise; get up; Stand up; draw out	溪 (Xī): Stream; Brook; rivulet
642	Yi Ying Shangguan	上官薏赢	Shàngguān Yì Yíng	薏 (Yì): The heart of a lotus seed; Jobs tears	赢 (Yíng): Win; Beat
643	Xuan Nai Shangguan	上官旋耐	Shàngguān Xuàn Nài	旋 (Xuàn): Whirl; turn something on a lathe	耐 (Nài): Be able to bear; To endure
644	Wu Can Helian	赫连吴灿	Hèlián Wú Càn	吴 (Wú): Wu, a state in the Zhou Dynasty	灿 (Càn): Bright; Illuminating
645	Ning Xuan Shentu	申屠宁旋	Shēntú Níng Xuán	宁 (Níng): Peaceful; tranquil	旋 (Xuán): Revolve; circle; spin; return; Soon
646	Xuan Xi Linghu	令狐旋熙	Lìnghú Xuàn Xī	旋 (Xuàn): Whirl; turn something on a lathe	熙 (Xī): Bright; sunny; prosperous
647	Pin Lu Gongyang	公羊品六	Gōngyáng Pǐn Lù	品 (Pǐn): Article; product; grade; class	六 (Lù): Used in place names;
648	Zhi Jie Zaifu	宰父志婕	Zǎifǔ Zhì Jié	志 (Zhì): Aspiration; ambition; Ideal;	婕 (Jié): Handsome; Beautiful

				will	
649	Nai Lian Yuezheng	乐正耐莲	Yuèzhèng Nài Lián	耐 (Nài): Be able to bear or endure; Tolerance	莲 (Lián): Lotus;
650	Ying Yan Chanyu	单于莹彦	Chányú Yíng Yàn	莹 (Yíng): Jade-like stone; Lustrous and transparent	彦 (Yàn): A man of virtue and ability; A surname
651	Huan Ping Shentu	申屠欢萍	Shēntú Huān Píng	欢 (Huān): Joyous; merry; Jubilant; vigorously	萍 (Píng): Duckweed;
652	Li Song Sikou	司寇莉宋	Sīkòu Lì Sòng	莉 (Lì): Jasmine; Jasmine flower	宋 (Sòng): Song, a state in the Zhou Dynasty
653	Xuan Xi Zongzheng	宗政璇曦	Zōngzhèng Xuán Xī	璇 (Xuán): Fine jade;	曦 (Xī): Sunlight (usually of early morning);
654	Fang Na Qiguan	亓官放娜	Qíguān Fàng Nà	放 (Fàng): Release; Set free	娜 (Nà): A word used in feminine names;
655	Xiao Jie Nangong	南宫肖婕	Nángōng Xiào Jié	肖 (Xiào): Resemble; Be like	婕 (Jié): Handsome; Beautiful
656	Xin Xiao Ouyang	欧阳欣肖	Ōuyáng Xīn Xiào	欣 (Xīn): Glad; Happy	肖 (Xiào): Resemble; Be like
657	Can Hua Nanmen	南门灿骅	Nánmén Càn Huá	灿 (Càn): Bright; Illuminating	骅 (Huá): Hualiu; Name of a famous horse
658	Wen Ya Zhongli	钟离雯丫	Zhōnglí Wén Yā	雯 (Wén): Cloud in beautiful patterns;	丫 (Yā): Ah; Bifurcation
659	Ge Xian Tantai	澹台歌娴	Tántái Gē Xián	歌 (Gē): Song; Sing	娴 (Xián): Refined; Skilled
660	Zhi Nai Zhuge	诸葛志耐	Zhūgě Zhì Nài	志 (Zhì): Aspiration; ambition; Ideal; will	耐 (Nài): Be able to bear; To endure
661	Nai Yi	亓官耐怡	Qíguān	耐 (Nài): Be able to	怡 (Yí): Happy;

			Qiguan		Nài Yí	bear; To endure	Joyful

662	Ping Jing Sikou	司寇萍静	Sīkòu Píng Jìng	萍 (Píng): Duckweed;	静 (Jìng): Still; Calm
663	Qi Sha Zhongsun	仲孙起沙	Zhòngsūn Qǐ Shā	起 (Qǐ): Rise; get up; Stand up; draw out	沙 (Shā): Sand; granulated; powdered; Hoarse
664	Hui Su Duanmu	端木惠苏	Duānmù Huì Sū	惠 (Huì): Favor; kindness; benefit; Favor; give	苏 (Sū): Revive; come to; Short for Suzhou; short for Jiangsu Province;
665	Nai Lian Dongfang	东方耐莲	Dōngfāng Nài Lián	耐 (Nài): Be able to bear; To endure	莲 (Lián): Lotus;
666	Jing Chun Zhongli	钟离京纯	Zhōnglí Jīng Chún	京 (Jīng): The capital of a country; Short for Beijing	纯 (Chún): Pure; Simple
667	Yi Nai Xuanyuan	轩辕艺耐	Xuānyuán Yì Nài	艺 (Yì): Art; Skill; norm; standard	耐 (Nài): Be able to bear; To endure
668	Qi Xun Zongzheng	宗政起勋	Zōngzhèng Qǐ Xūn	起 (Qǐ): Rise; get up; Stand up; draw out	勋 (Xūn): Merit; Meritorious service
669	Wan Xing Zhongsun	仲孙婉幸	Zhòngsūn Wǎn Xìng	婉 (Wǎn): Tactful; polite; Gracious; gentle and agreeable	幸 (Xìng): Good fortune; favor
670	Xue Ying Ouyang	欧阳雪瀛	Ōuyáng Xuě Yíng	雪 (Xuě): Snow; Wipe out	瀛 (Yíng): Ocean; Sea
671	Zhou Pin Dongguo	东郭周品	Dōngguō Zhōu Pǐn	周 (Zhōu): Circumference; periphery; circuit; week	品 (Pǐn): Article; product; grade; class
672	Mei Yi Diwu	第五梅意	Dìwǔ Méi Yì	梅 (Méi): Plum; Prunus mume	意 (Yì): Meaning; idea; Wish; desire
673	Ling Fang Tantai	澹台令方	Tántái Lǐng Fāng	令 (Lǐng): Ream;	方 (Fāng): Square; involution
674	Yi Xia	公冶怡霞	Gōngyě Yí	怡 (Yí): Happy;	霞 (Xiá): Rosy

			Gongye		Xiá	Joyful	clouds; Morning or evening glow
675	Tian Qing Ximen	西门甜晴	Xīmén Tián Qíng	甜 (Tián): Sweetness; Sweet; honeyed	晴 (Qíng): Clear; Fine
676	Lu Xi Moqi	万俟露熙	Mòqí Lù Xī	露 (Lù): Dew; syrup; fruit juice	熙 (Xī): Bright; sunny; prosperous
677	Miao Wen Gongye	公冶苗雯	Gōngyě Miáo Wén	苗 (Miáo): Seedling; Sprout;	雯 (Wén): Cloud in beautiful patterns;
678	Xiao Chun Baili	百里肖淳	Bǎilǐ Xiāo Chún	肖 (Xiāo): A surname;	淳 (Chún): Pure; Honest
679	Su Xian Shentu	申屠苏娴	Shēntú Sū Xián	苏 (Sū): Revive; come to; Short for Suzhou; short for Jiangsu Province;	娴 (Xián): Refined; Skilled
680	Xin Ying Ziju	子车心莹	Zǐjū Xīn Yíng	心 (Xīn): The heart; Mind	莹 (Yíng): Jade-like stone; Lustrous and transparent
681	An Jin Zhongli	钟离庵觐	Zhōnglí Ān Jìn	庵 (Ān): Nunnery; Buddhist convent	觐 (Jìn): Present oneself before; Go on a pilgrimage
682	Yan Ya Diwu	第五燕娅	Dìwǔ Yàn Yà	燕 (Yàn): Swallow; Feast	娅 (Yà): Ya, used in name; Husbands of sisters
683	Ying Yuan Qidiao	漆雕莹媛	Qīdiāo Yíng Yuán	莹 (Yíng): Jade-like stone; Lustrous and transparent	媛 (Yuán): Pretty (used in female names);
684	Duo Ling Linghu	令狐朵灵	Lìnghú Duǒ Líng	朵 (Duǒ): Flower; A surname	灵 (Líng): Quick; clever
685	Miao Lian Wenren	闻人苗莲	Wénrén Miáo Lián	苗 (Miáo): Seedling; Sprout;	莲 (Lián): Lotus;
686	Wei Shi Zhongsun	仲孙蔚是	Zhòngsūn Wèi Shì	蔚 (Wèi): Luxuriant; Grand	是 (Shì): Yes; correct; right; true
687	Chun Nai Rangsi	壤驷淳耐	Rǎngsì Chún Nài	淳 (Chún): Pure; Honest	耐 (Nài): Be able to bear or endure; Tolerance

688	Xiao Shi Linghu	令狐肖是	Lìnghú Xiào Shì	肖 (Xiào): Resemble; Be like	是 (Shì): Yes; correct; right
689	Jing Wei Zhangdu	仉督静薇	Zhǎngdū Jìng Wēi	静 (Jìng): Still; Calm	薇 (Wēi): Common vetch; Vicia sativa
690	Han Ying Duanmu	端木寒滢	Duānmù Hán Yíng	寒 (Hán): Cold; Afraid; fearful	滢 (Yíng): Crystal-clear;
691	Ying Mei Zhuge	诸葛颖梅	Zhūgě Yǐng Méi	颖 (Yǐng): Grain husk; Glume; tip; point	梅 (Méi): Plum; Prunus mume
692	Huan Ling Zhuge	诸葛欢铃	Zhūgě Huān Líng	欢 (Huān): Joyous; merry; Jubilant; vigorously	铃 (Líng): Bell; boll; Bud
693	Nuo Zhi Zhangsun	长孙诺芝	Zhǎngsūn Nuò Zhī	诺 (Nuò): Promise; Yes	芝 (Zhī): A surname; Glossy ganoderma
694	Zhuo Ning Duanmu	端木卓宁	Duānmù Zhuō Nìng	卓 (Zhuō): Tall and erect; Upright	宁 (Nìng): Rather; Would rather
695	Nuan Yan Dongguo	东郭暖妍	Dōngguō Nuǎn Yán	暖 (Nuǎn): Warm; Genial	妍 (Yán): Beautiful;
696	Yan Yi Xianyu	鲜于彦怡	Xiānyú Yàn Yí	彦 (Yàn): Elegant; accomplished	怡 (Yí): Happy; Joyful
697	Miao Zhou Diwu	第五苗周	Dìwǔ Miáo Zhōu	苗 (Miáo): Seedling; Sprout;	周 (Zhōu): Circumference; periphery; circuit; week
698	Ting Yi Rangsi	壤驷婷懿	Rǎngsì Tíng Yì	婷 (Tíng): Graceful;	懿 (Yì): Exemplary; A virtuous woman
699	Xin Ling Nangong	南宫馨玲	Nángōng Xīn Líng	馨 (Xīn): Strong and pervasive fragrance;	玲 (Líng): Sound of jade;
700	Jin Yue Zhongli	钟离觐玥	Zhōnglí Jìn Yuè	觐 (Jìn): Present oneself before; Go on a pilgrimage	玥 (Yuè): A legendary supernatural pearl in ancient China;

701	Hua Wen Sikou	司寇骅雯	Sīkòu Huá Wén	骅 (Huá): Hualiu; Name of a famous horse	雯 (Wén): Cloud in beautiful patterns;
702	Zhan Huan Llvqu	闾丘瞻环	Lǘqiū Zhān Huán	瞻 (Zhān): Look forward or up;	环 (Huán): Ring; hoop; link; Surround;
703	Ying Fang Gongyang	公羊赢方	Gōngyáng Yíng Fāng	赢 (Yíng): Win; Beat	方 (Fāng): Square; involution
704	Na Qiong Zhongli	钟离娜琼	Zhōnglí Nà Qióng	娜 (Nà): A word used in feminine names;	琼 (Qióng): Fine jade;
705	Ying Qin Diwu	第五迎琴	Dìwǔ Yíng Qín	迎 (Yíng): Welcome; Greet	琴 (Qín): Qin, a seven-stringed plucked instrument
706	Dian Yan Shangguan	上官典燕	Shàngguān Diǎn Yān	典 (Diǎn): Standard; law; canon	燕 (Yān): A surname; North Hebei
707	Shu Nai Ximen	西门淑耐	Xīmén Shū Nài	淑 (Shū): Kind and gentle; Fair	耐 (Nài): Be able to bear; To endure
708	Yu Ning Sikong	司空瑜宁	Sīkōng Yú Nìng	瑜 (Yú): Yoga; Fine jade; gem	宁 (Nìng): Rather; Would rather
709	Ying Dai Qiguan	亓官颖代	Qíguān Yǐng Dài	颖 (Yǐng): Grain husk; Glume; tip; point	代 (Dài): Take the place of
710	Bai Wu Sikong	司空百伍	Sīkōng Bǎi Wǔ	百 (Bǎi): Surname; Hundred	伍 (Wǔ): Five
711	Ying Jie Shentu	申屠赢婕	Shēntú Yíng Jié	赢 (Yíng): Win; Beat	婕 (Jié): Handsome; Beautiful
712	Dong Wan Taishu	太叔冬婉	Tàishū Dōng Wǎn	冬 (Dōng): Winter; Rub-a-	婉 (Wǎn): Tactful; polite; Gracious;

				dub	gentle and agreeable
713	Qin Han Ouyang	欧阳琴寒	Ōuyáng Qín Hán	琴 (Qín): Qin, a seven-stringed plucked instrument	寒 (Hán): Cold; Afraid; fearful
714	Yin Nuan Huyan	呼延崟暖	Hūyán Yín Nuǎn	崟 (Yín): High and steep;	暖 (Nuǎn): Warm; Genial
715	Xiao Zhi Zhuansun	颛孙肖芝	Zhuānsūn Xiào Zhī	肖 (Xiào): Resemble; Be like	芝 (Zhī): A surname; Glossy ganoderma
716	Dong Wei Nangong	南宫冬薇	Nángōng Dōng Wēi	冬 (Dōng): Winter; Rub-a-dub	薇 (Wēi): Common vetch; Vicia sativa
717	Yi Zhi Murong	慕容仪志	Mùróng Yí Zhì	仪 (Yí): Instrument; Meter; bearing	志 (Zhì): Aspiration; ambition; Ideal; will
718	Yue Xi Gongye	公冶玥溪	Gōngyě Yuè Xī	玥 (Yuè): A legendary supernatural pearl in ancient China;	溪 (Xī): Stream; Brook; rivulet
719	Can Xi Ziju	子车灿曦	Zǐjū Càn Xī	灿 (Càn): Bright; Illuminating	曦 (Xī): The sunrise; (Usually of early morning) sunlight
720	Ling Xuan Situ	司徒令旋	Sītú Lìng Xuàn	令 (Lìng): Order; command; decree	旋 (Xuàn): Whirl; turn something on a lathe
721	Dian Xi Murong	慕容典曦	Mùróng Diǎn Xī	典 (Diǎn): Standard; law; canon	曦 (Xī): The sunrise; (Usually of early morning) sunlight
722	Sha Bai Duangan	段干沙百	Duàngān Shà Bǎi	沙 (Shà): Shake;	百 (Bǎi): All; all kinds of; classes

723	Yu Xian Ouyang	欧阳语娴	Ōuyáng Yǔ Xián	语 (Yǔ): Language; tongue; Words; set phrase	娴 (Xián): Refined; Skilled
724	Man Fen Ximen	西门曼芬	Xīmén Màn Fēn	曼 (Màn): Graceful; Soft and beautiful	芬 (Fēn): Sweet smell; Fragrance
725	Xi Wu Gongsun	公孙曦伍	Gōngsūn Xī Wǔ	曦 (Xī): The sunrise; (Usually of early morning) sunlight	伍 (Wǔ): Five
726	Nai Zi Situ	司徒耐姿	Sītú Nài Zī	耐 (Nài): Be able to bear or endure; Tolerance	姿 (Zī): Posture; Looks; appearance
727	Shi Lian Yuchi	尉迟是联	Yùchí Shì Lián	是 (Shì): Yes; correct; right; true; Praise; justify	联 (Lián): Unite; Join
728	Hui Yu Dongmen	东门慧于	Dōngmén Huì Yú	慧 (Huì): Wisdom; Intelligent	于 (Yú): Denotes time, location, scope, etc.
729	Ying Ge Duanmu	端木莹歌	Duānmù Yíng Gē	莹 (Yíng): Jade-like stone; Lustrous and transparent	歌 (Gē): Song; Sing
730	Qin Lu Gongliang	公良琴六	Gōngliáng Qín Lù	琴 (Qín): Qin, a seven-stringed plucked instrument	六 (Lù): Used in place names;
731	Yu An Moqi	万俟语庵	Mòqí Yù Ān	语 (Yù): Tell; Inform	庵 (Ān): Nunnery; Buddhist convent
732	Pei ga Zuoqiu	左丘培伽	Zuǒqiū Péi gā	培 (Péi): Training; cultivate; Earth up; foster	伽 (gā): Gamma;
733	Xi Qin	巫马溪琴	Wūmǎ Xī	溪 (Xī): Stream;	琴 (Qín): Qin, a

	Wuma		Qín	Brook; rivulet	seven-stringed plucked instrument
734	Shi Sha Ouyang	欧阳诗莎	Ōuyáng Shī Shā	诗 (Shī): Poem; poetry; Verse	莎 (Shā): Personal and place names
735	Xin Jiao Yuezheng	乐正欣娇	Yuèzhèng Xīn Jiāo	欣 (Xīn): Glad; Happy	娇 (Jiāo): Tender; Lovely
736	Sha Jing Rangsi	壤驷沙静	Rǎngsì Shā Jìng	沙 (Shā): Sand; granulated; powdered; Hoarse	静 (Jìng): Still; Calm
737	Nuan Wu Zhuge	诸葛暖伍	Zhūgě Nuǎn Wǔ	暖 (Nuǎn): Warm; Genial	伍 (Wǔ): Five
738	Yue Chang Guliang	榖梁玥畅	Gǔliáng Yuè Chàng	玥 (Yuè): A legendary supernatural pearl in ancient China;	畅 (Chàng): Smooth; unimpeded; Free
739	Hui Huan Dongmen	东门惠欢	Dōngmén Huì Huān	惠 (Huì): Favor; kindness; benefit; Favor; give	欢 (Huān): Joyous; merry; Jubilant; vigorously
740	Jing Ya Xiahou	夏侯靖娅	Xiàhóu Jìng Yà	靖 (Jìng): Peaceful; Tranquil	娅 (Yà): Ya, used in name; Husbands of sisters
741	Yan Zhi Liangqiu	梁丘艳芝	Liángqiū Yàn Zhī	艳 (Yàn): Gorgeous; colorful; Gaudy; amorous	芝 (Zhī): A surname; Glossy ganoderma
742	Tong Wei Huangpu	皇甫彤薇	Huángpǔ Tóng Wēi	彤 (Tóng): Red; Vermilion	薇 (Wēi): Common vetch; Vicia sativa
743	Zhi Wan Chunyu	淳于芝婉	Chúnyú Zhī Wǎn	芝 (Zhī): A surname; Glossy ganoderma	婉 (Wǎn): Tactful; polite; Gracious; gentle and agreeable
744	Yi Lian Baili	百里忆莲	Bǎilǐ Yì	忆 (Yì): Recall;	莲 (Lián): Lotus;

			Lián	Recollect	
745	Chun Xing Zhangdu	仉督淳幸	Zhǎngdū Chún Xìng	淳 (Chún): Pure; Honest	幸 (Xìng): Good fortune; favor
746	Bai Qing Guliang	穀梁百晴	Gǔliáng Bǎi Qíng	百 (Bǎi): Surname; Hundred	晴 (Qíng): Clear; Fine
747	Nuan Yin Murong	慕容暖崟	Mùróng Nuǎn Yín	暖 (Nuǎn): Warm; Genial	崟 (Yín): High and steep;
748	Yao Ya Liangqiu	梁丘瑶雅	Liángqiū Yáo Yǎ	瑶 (Yáo): Precious jade; A surname	雅 (Yǎ): Refined; elegant; standard
749	Nai Chang Puyang	濮阳耐畅	Púyáng Nài Chàng	耐 (Nài): Be able to bear; To endure	畅 (Chàng): Smooth; unimpeded; Free
750	Qin Nai Dongfang	东方勤奈	Dōngfāng Qín Nài	勤 (Qín): Diligent; industrious; Hardworking; often	奈 (Nài): But; however; Tackle; deal with; bear stand
751	Zhuo Jia Ziju	子车卓伽	Zǐjū Zhuō Jiā	卓 (Zhuō): Table; Desk	伽 (Jiā): Korean musical instrument;
752	Lian Xue Gongliang	公良莲雪	Gōngliáng Lián Xuě	莲 (Lián): Lotus;	雪 (Xuě): Snow; Wipe out
753	Tao Ying Gongxi	公西桃赢	Gōngxī Táo Yíng	桃 (Táo): Peach; Peach-shaped things	赢 (Yíng): Win; Beat
754	Ge Xin Chunyu	淳于歌馨	Chúnyú Gē Xīn	歌 (Gē): Song; Sing	馨 (Xīn): Strong and pervasive fragrance;
755	Ling Xin Shentu	申屠令馨	Shēntú Lìng Xīn	令 (Lìng): Order; command; decree	馨 (Xīn): Strong and pervasive fragrance;
756	Yu Ze Taishu	太叔愚则	Tàishū Yú Zé	愚 (Yú): I; Make a fool of; fool	则 (Zé): Standard; norm; criterion
757	Ya Zhi Helian	赫连雅志	Hèlián Yǎ Zhì	雅 (Yǎ): Refined; elegant;	志 (Zhì): Aspiration;

				standard; proper	ambition
758	Ying Yan Llvqu	闾丘迎燕	Lǘqiū Yíng Yàn	迎 (Yíng): Welcome; Greet	燕 (Yàn): Swallow; Feast
759	Xi Dai Yuezheng	乐正溪代	Yuèzhèng Xī Dài	溪 (Xī): Stream; Brook; rivulet	代 (Dài): Take the place of
760	Xin Ying Sima	司马欣莹	Sīmǎ Xīn Yíng	欣 (Xīn): Glad; Happy	莹 (Yíng): Jade-like stone; Lustrous and transparent
761	Yue Yuan Dongguo	东郭悦媛	Dōngguō Yuè Yuán	悦 (Yuè): Happy; Pleased	媛 (Yuán): Pretty (used in female names);
762	Xi Ling Dongmen	东门溪令	Dōngmén Xī Lǐng	溪 (Xī): Stream; Brook; rivulet	令 (Lǐng): Ream;
763	Yi Xuan Sima	司马仪璇	Sīmǎ Yí Xuán	仪 (Yí): Instrument; Meter; bearing	璇 (Xuán): Fine jade;
764	Ling Su Wenren	闻人灵苏	Wénrén Líng Sū	灵 (Líng): Quick; clever; Bright; effective	苏 (Sū): Revive; come to; Short for Suzhou; short for Jiangsu Province;
765	Yan ga Xiahou	夏侯燕伽	Xiàhóu Yān gā	燕 (Yān): A surname; North Hebei	伽 (gā): Gamma;
766	Qin Liu Guliang	榖梁勤六	Gǔliáng Qín Liù	勤 (Qín): Diligent; industrious; Hardworking; often	六 (Liù): Six; 6; number six
767	Ting Dian Zongzheng	宗政婷典	Zōngzhèng Tíng Diǎn	婷 (Tíng): Graceful;	典 (Diǎn): Standard; law; canon
768	Jin Yuan Yuezheng	乐正觐缘	Yuèzhèng Jìn Yuán	觐 (Jìn): Present oneself before; Go on a pilgrimage	缘 (Yuán): Reason; predestined relationship
769	Qin Zhi Situ	司徒琴志	Sītú Qín Zhì	琴 (Qín): Qin, a seven-stringed	志 (Zhì): Aspiration;

				plucked instrument	ambition; Ideal; will
770	Yu Zhuo Dongfang	东方瑜卓	Dōngfāng Yú Zhuō	瑜 (Yú): Yoga; Fine jade; gem	卓 (Zhuō): Tall and erect; Upright
771	Yu Yan Ximen	西门于颜	Xīmén Yú Yán	于 (Yú): Denotes time, location, scope, etc.	颜 (Yán): Face; Countenance
772	Ze Qiong Xianyu	鲜于则琼	Xiānyú Zé Qióng	则 (Zé): Standard; norm; criterion	琼 (Qióng): Fine jade;
773	An Yang Jiagu	夹谷庵洋	Jiágǔ Ān Yáng	庵 (Ān): Nunnery; Buddhist convent	洋 (Yáng): Ocean; silver coin; Vast; multitudinous
774	Shi Lian Chunyu	淳于是联	Chúnyú Shì Lián	是 (Shì): Yes; correct; right; true; Praise; justify	联 (Lián): Unite; Join
775	Ying Xuan Gongliang	公良迎旋	Gōngliáng Yíng Xuàn	迎 (Yíng): Welcome; Greet	旋 (Xuàn): Whirl; turn something on a lathe
776	Xia ou Puyang	濮阳霞欧	Púyáng Xiá Ōu	霞 (Xiá): Rosy clouds; Morning or evening glow	欧 (Ōu): Short for Europe; A surname
777	Jing Yuan Chunyu	淳于靖媛	Chúnyú Jìng Yuán	靖 (Jìng): Peaceful; Tranquil	媛 (Yuán): Pretty (used in female names);
778	Xue Tong Xiahou	夏侯雪彤	Xiàhóu Xuě Tóng	雪 (Xuě): Snow; Wipe out	彤 (Tóng): Red; Vermilion
779	Ying Huan Tantai	澹台瀛环	Tántái Yíng Huán	瀛 (Yíng): Ocean; Sea	环 (Huán): Ring; hoop; link; Surround;
780	Miao Qin Situ	司徒苗琴	Sītú Miáo Qín	苗 (Miáo): Seedling; Sprout;	琴 (Qín): Qin, a seven-stringed plucked instrument
781	Su Ling	宗政苏灵	Zōngzhèng	苏 (Sū): Revive;	灵 (Líng): Quick;

			Sū Líng	come to; Short for Suzhou; short for Jiangsu Province;	clever; Bright; effective
Zongzheng					
782	Dong Wei Situ	司徒冬蔚	Sītú Dōng Wèi	冬 (Dōng): Winter; Rub-a-dub	蔚 (Wèi): Luxuriant; Grand
783	Yu Han Llvqu	闾丘雨寒	Lǘqiū Yǔ Hán	雨 (Yǔ): Rain; Wet	寒 (Hán): Cold; Afraid; fearful
784	Qin Jin Zuoqiu	左丘琴槿	Zuǒqiū Qín Jǐn	琴 (Qín): Qin, a seven-stringed plucked instrument	槿 (Jǐn): Hibiscus; Rose of Sharon
785	Xin Dong Gongyang	公羊馨冬	Gōngyáng Xīn Dōng	馨 (Xīn): Strong and pervasive fragrance;	冬 (Dōng): Winter; Rub-a-dub
786	Tong Xin Linghu	令狐彤昕	Lìnghú Tóng Xīn	彤 (Tóng): Red; Vermilion	昕 (Xīn): Day; Sunrise
787	Yan Liu Yuezheng	乐正彦六	Yuèzhèng Yàn Liù	彦 (Yàn): A man of virtue and ability; A surname	六 (Liù): Six; 6; number six
788	Xuan Yan Chanyu	单于旋彦	Chányú Xuán Yàn	旋 (Xuán): Revolve; circle; spin; return; Soon	彦 (Yàn): A man of virtue and ability; A surname
789	Dian Yin Ziju	子车典崟	Zǐjū Diǎn Yín	典 (Diǎn): Standard; law; canon	崟 (Yín): High and steep;
790	Wu Yin Moqi	万俟吴崟	Mòqí Wú Yín	吴 (Wú): Wu, a state in the Zhou Dynasty	崟 (Yín): High and steep;
791	Sha Ling Huyan	呼延沙令	Hūyán Shà Líng	沙 (Shà): Shake;	令 (Líng): A surname;
792	Ling Ping Dongfang	东方铃萍	Dōngfāng Líng Píng	铃 (Líng): Bell; boll; Bud	萍 (Píng): Duckweed;

793	Miao Yun Zuoqiu	左丘苗匀	Zuǒqiū Miáo Yún	苗 (Miáo): Seedling; Sprout;	匀 (Yún): Uniform; Even
794	Meng Xi Zhongli	钟离梦喜	Zhōnglí Mèng Xǐ	梦 (Mèng): Dream;	喜 (Xǐ): Be happy; be delighted; Be pleased; be fond of
795	Miao Juan Zhuansun	颛孙淼娟	Zhuānsūn Miǎo Juān	淼 (Miǎo): Vast; Wide expanse of water	娟 (Juān): Graceful; Beautiful
796	Huan Feng Diwu	第五欢枫	Dìwǔ Huān Fēng	欢 (Huān): Joyous; merry; Jubilant; vigorously	枫 (Fēng): Maple; Chinese sweet gum
797	Bai Ling Zhongli	钟离百令	Zhōnglí Bǎi Lìng	百 (Bǎi): Surname; Hundred	令 (Lìng): Order; command; decree
798	An Hui Duangan	段干庵惠	Duàngān Ān Huì	庵 (Ān): Nunnery; Buddhist convent	惠 (Huì): Favor; kindness; benefit; Favor; give
799	Si Hui Situ	司徒兕慧	Sītú Sì Huì	兕 (Sì): Female rhinoceros;	慧 (Huì): Wisdom; Intelligent
800	Nai Ruo Sikong	司空耐若	Sīkōng Nài Ruò	耐 (Nài): Be able to bear or endure; Tolerance	若 (Ruò): Like; seem; As if

801	Sha Ze Gongyang	公羊莎则	Gōngyáng Shā Zé	莎 (Shā): Personal and place names	则 (Zé): Standard; norm; criterion
802	Lian Li Wuma	巫马莲丽	Wūmǎ Lián Lí	莲 (Lián): Lotus;	丽 (Lí): Meet with;
803	Qi Sha Situ	司徒起沙	Sītú Qǐ Shā	起 (Qǐ): Rise; get up; Stand up; draw out	沙 (Shā): Sand; granulated; powdered; Hoarse
804	Can Yi Jiagu	夹谷灿薏	Jiágǔ Càn Yì	灿 (Càn): Bright; Illuminating	薏 (Yì): The heart of a lotus seed; Jobs tears
805	Fang Yuan Zhuge	诸葛放缘	Zhūgě Fàng Yuán	放 (Fàng): Release; Set free	缘 (Yuán): Reason; predestined relationship
806	Zhi Yi Dongguo	东郭志懿	Dōngguō Zhì Yì	志 (Zhì): Aspiration; ambition	懿 (Yì): Exemplary; A virtuous woman
807	Ying Xun Yuchi	尉迟莹勋	Yùchí Yíng Xūn	莹 (Yíng): Jade-like stone; Lustrous and transparent	勋 (Xūn): Merit; Meritorious service
808	Nuo Tian Shangguan	上官诺甜	Shàngguān Nuò Tián	诺 (Nuò): Promise; Yes	甜 (Tián): Sweetness; Sweet; honeyed
809	Yuan Yang Zhangsun	长孙缘扬	Zhǎngsūn Yuán Yáng	缘 (Yuán): Reason; predestined relationship	扬 (Yáng): Raise; throw up and scatter; Winnow; spread
810	Chi Qing Linghu	令狐驰晴	Lìnghú Chí Qíng	驰 (Chí): Speed; Turn eagerly towards	晴 (Qíng): Clear; Fine

811	Wu Xin Shentu	申屠吴心	Shēntú Wú Xīn	吴 (Wú): Wu, a state in the Zhou Dynasty	心 (Xīn): The heart; Mind
812	Qi Yan Zongzheng	宗政起彦	Zōngzhèng Qǐ Yàn	起 (Qǐ): Rise; get up; Stand up; draw out	彦 (Yàn): A man of virtue and ability; A surname
813	Xuan Zhuo Rangsi	壤驷旋卓	Rǎngsì Xuàn Zhuō	旋 (Xuàn): Whirl; turn something on a lathe	卓 (Zhuō): Table; Desk
814	Yu Man Xiahou	夏侯语曼	Xiàhóu Yǔ Màn	语 (Yǔ): Language; tongue; Words; set phrase	曼 (Màn): Graceful; Soft and beautiful
815	Dai Bai Jiagu	夹谷代百	Jiágǔ Dài Bǎi	代 (Dài): Take the place of	百 (Bǎi): All; all kinds of; classes
816	Juan Jing Qidiao	漆雕娟泾	Qīdiāo Juān Jīng	娟 (Juān): Graceful; Beautiful	泾 (Jīng): Short for the Jinghe River;
817	Wei Ling Sikou	司寇薇铃	Sīkòu Wēi Líng	薇 (Wēi): Common vetch; Vicia sativa	铃 (Líng): Bell; boll; Bud
818	Xin Feng Zhongsun	仲孙昕枫	Zhòngsūn Xīn Fēng	昕 (Xīn): Day; Sunrise	枫 (Fēng): Maple; Chinese sweet gum
819	Ning Wan Zuoqiu	左丘宁曼	Zuǒqiū Níng Wàn	宁 (Níng): Peaceful; tranquil	曼 (Wàn): A surname;
820	Ning Bai Yuwen	宇文宁百	Yǔwén Níng Bǎi	宁 (Níng): Peaceful; tranquil	百 (Bǎi): All; all kinds of; classes
821	Xuan Yi Yuchi	尉迟旋薏	Yùchí Xuán Yì	旋 (Xuán): Revolve; circle; spin; return; Soon	薏 (Yì): The heart of a lotus seed; Jobs tears
822	Xi Xian Xuanyuan	轩辕溪娴	Xuānyuán Xī Xián	溪 (Xī): Stream; Brook; rivulet	娴 (Xián): Refined; Skilled
823	Xian Yu Sikong	司空娴昱	Sīkōng Xián Yù	娴 (Xián): Refined; Skilled	昱 (Yù): Sunlight; Sunshine
824	Nai Wei Xiahou	夏侯耐薇	Xiàhóu Nài Wēi	耐 (Nài): Be able to bear or endure; Tolerance	薇 (Wēi): Common vetch; Vicia sativa

825	Xuan Jin Helian	赫连璇觐	Hèlián Xuán Jìn	璇 (Xuán): Fine jade;	觐 (Jìn): Present oneself before; Go on a pilgrimage
826	Zi Sha Zhuansun	颛孙姿沙	Zhuānsūn Zī Shā	姿 (Zī): Posture; Looks; appearance	沙 (Shā): Sand; granulated; powdered; Hoarse
827	Zhou Yan Moqi	万俟周艳	Mòqí Zhōu Yàn	周 (Zhōu): Circumference; periphery; circuit; week	艳 (Yàn): Gorgeous; colorful; Gaudy; amorous
828	Xiao Wu Yuwen	宇文肖伍	Yǔwén Xiāo Wǔ	肖 (Xiāo): A surname;	伍 (Wǔ): Five
829	Ying Chun Yuchi	尉迟滢纯	Yùchí Yíng Chún	滢 (Yíng): Crystal-clear;	纯 (Chún): Pure; Simple
830	ou Ya Puyang	濮阳欧雅	Púyáng Ōu Yǎ	欧 (Ōu): Short for Europe; A surname	雅 (Yǎ): Refined; elegant; standard; proper
831	Xiao ga Yangshe	羊舌肖伽	Yángshé Xiào gā	肖 (Xiào): Resemble; Be like	伽 (gā): Gamma;
832	Duo Bai Tuoba	拓跋多百	Tuòbá Duō Bǎi	多 (Duō): Many; much; more	百 (Bǎi): Surname; Hundred
833	Yi Zhao Situ	司徒艺昭	Sītú Yì Zhāo	艺 (Yì): Art; Skill; norm; standard	昭 (Zhāo): Show; Manifest
834	Xi Rui Nanmen	南门熙瑞	Nánmén Xī Ruì	熙 (Xī): Bright; sunny; prosperous	瑞 (Ruì): Auspicious; lucky
835	Huan Bai Chanyu	单于欢百	Chányú Huān Bǎi	欢 (Huān): Joyous; merry; Jubilant; vigorously	百 (Bǎi): All; all kinds of; classes
836	Yang Ying Zhangdu	仉督扬赢	Zhǎngdū Yáng Yíng	扬 (Yáng): Raise; throw up and scatter; Winnow; spread	赢 (Yíng): Win; Beat
837	Yu Xia	羊舌蔚霞	Yángshé	蔚 (Yù): A surname;	霞 (Xiá): Rosy

	Yangshe		Yù Xiá		clouds; Morning or evening glow
838	Sha Ya Moqi	万俟莎丫	Mòqí Shā Yā	莎 (Shā): Personal and place names	丫 (Yā): Ah; Bifurcation
839	Liu Jing Puyang	濮阳六京	Púyáng Liù Jīng	六 (Liù): Six; 6; number six	京 (Jīng): The capital of a country; Short for Beijing
840	Zhao Sha Gongsun	公孙昭沙	Gōngsūn Zhāo Shā	昭 (Zhāo): Show; Manifest	沙 (Shā): Sand; granulated; powdered; Hoarse
841	Xue Yi Chanyu	单于雪怡	Chányú Xuě Yí	雪 (Xuě): Snow; Wipe out	怡 (Yí): Happy; Joyful
842	Jin Yun Gongsun	公孙觐匀	Gōngsūn Jìn Yún	觐 (Jìn): Present oneself before; Go on a pilgrimage	匀 (Yún): Uniform; Even
843	Meng Fang Nanmen	南门梦放	Nánmén Mèng Fàng	梦 (Mèng): Dream;	放 (Fàng): Release; Set free
844	Bai Xi Duanmu	端木百曦	Duānmù Bǎi Xī	百 (Bǎi): Surname; Hundred	曦 (Xī): The sunrise; (Usually of early morning) sunlight
845	Yue Si Dongmen	东门月兕	Dōngmén Yuè Sì	月 (Yuè): Moon; Month	兕 (Sì): Female rhinoceros;
846	Yin Ying Zhangsun	长孙崟滢	Zhǎngsūn Yín Yíng	崟 (Yín): High and steep;	滢 (Yíng): Crystal-clear;
847	Yu Qing Xianyu	鲜于语晴	Xiānyú Yù Qíng	语 (Yù): Tell; Inform	晴 (Qíng): Clear; Fine
848	Nai Jin Xianyu	鲜于耐觐	Xiānyú Nài Jìn	耐 (Nài): Be able to bear; To endure	觐 (Jìn): Present oneself before; Go on a pilgrimage
849	Wan Feng Llvqu	闾丘曼枫	Lǘqiū Wàn Fēng	曼 (Wàn): A surname;	枫 (Fēng): Maple; Chinese

					sweet gum
850	Wan ga Zhuge	诸葛婉伽	Zhūgě Wǎn gā	婉 (Wǎn): Tactful; polite; Gracious; gentle and agreeable	伽 (gā): Gamma;
851	Ying Jin Gongye	公冶赢觐	Gōngyě Yíng Jìn	赢 (Yíng): Win; Beat	觐 (Jìn): Present oneself before; Go on a pilgrimage
852	Zhen Xia Huyan	呼延真霞	Hūyán Zhēn Xiá	真 (Zhēn): Genuine; Real	霞 (Xiá): Rosy clouds; Morning or evening glow
853	Yun Chi Linghu	令狐匀驰	Lìnghú Yún Chí	匀 (Yún): Uniform; Even	驰 (Chí): Speed; Turn eagerly towards
854	Ling Li Yangshe	羊舌玲李	Yángshé Líng Lǐ	玲 (Líng): Sound of jade;	李 (Lǐ): Plum; A surname
855	Li Jie Duanmu	端木丽婕	Duānmù Lí Jié	丽 (Lí): Meet with;	婕 (Jié): Handsome; Beautiful
856	Xin Xi Gongliang	公良欣熙	Gōngliáng Xīn Xī	欣 (Xīn): Glad; Happy	熙 (Xī): Bright; sunny; prosperous
857	Ying Yuan Zhangsun	长孙滢媛	Zhǎngsūn Yíng Yuàn	滢 (Yíng): Crystal-clear;	媛 (Yuàn): Pretty girl; Beautiful women
858	Shi Xi Moqi	万俟是熙	Mòqí Shì Xī	是 (Shì): Yes; correct; right; true; Praise; justify	熙 (Xī): Bright; sunny; prosperous
859	Jing Ling Zhuge	诸葛静令	Zhūgě Jìng Lìng	静 (Jìng): Still; Calm	令 (Lìng): Order; command; decree
860	Ying Li Zongzheng	宗政赢丽	Zōngzhèng Yíng Lì	赢 (Yíng): Win; Beat	丽 (Lì): Beautiful; Pretty
861	Sha Nuo Helian	赫连莎诺	Hèlián Shā Nuò	莎 (Shā): Personal and place names	诺 (Nuò): Promise; Yes

862	Lu Ying Zhongsun	仲孙六瀛	Zhòngsūn Lù Yíng	六 (Lù): Used in place names;	瀛 (Yíng): Ocean; Sea
863	Ying Zhu Qidiao	漆雕滢珠	Qīdiāo Yíng Zhū	滢 (Yíng): Crystal-clear;	珠 (Zhū): Bead; Pearl
864	Yu Lian Helian	赫连昱联	Hèlián Yù Lián	昱 (Yù): Sunlight; Sunshine	联 (Lián): Unite; Join
865	Yuan Yi Gongxi	公西媛薏	Gōngxī Yuàn Yì	媛 (Yuàn): Pretty girl; Beautiful women	薏 (Yì): The heart of a lotus seed; Jobs tears
866	Si Dai Nangong	南宫兕代	Nángōng Sì Dài	兕 (Sì): Female rhinoceros;	代 (Dài): Take the place of
867	Ping Yi Dongguo	东郭萍仪	Dōngguō Píng Yí	萍 (Píng): Duckweed;	仪 (Yí): Instrument; Meter; bearing
868	Sha Yi Dongmen	东门沙忆	Dōngmén Shā Yì	沙 (Shā): Sand; granulated; powdered; Hoarse	忆 (Yì): Recall; Recollect
869	Ruo Fen Zhuansun	颛孙若芬	Zhuānsūn Ruò Fēn	若 (Ruò): Like; seem; As if	芬 (Fēn): Sweet smell; Fragrance
870	Miao Yin Shangguan	上官苗崟	Shàngguān Miáo Yín	苗 (Miáo): Seedling; Sprout;	崟 (Yín): High and steep;
871	Qin Xin Llvqu	闾丘琴馨	Lǘqiū Qín Xīn	琴 (Qín): Qin, a seven-stringed plucked instrument	馨 (Xīn): Strong and pervasive fragrance;
872	Nai Tong Zhangdu	仉督耐彤	Zhǎngdū Nài Tóng	耐 (Nài): Be able to bear; To endure	彤 (Tóng): Red; Vermilion
873	Ning Nuan Yangshe	羊舌宁暖	Yángshé Níng Nuǎn	宁 (Níng): Peaceful; tranquil	暖 (Nuǎn): Warm; Genial
874	Sha Jin Zhuge	诸葛莎觐	Zhūgě Shā Jìn	莎 (Shā): Personal and place names	觐 (Jìn): Present oneself before; Go on a pilgrimage
875	Dai Ying Yangshe	羊舌代迎	Yángshé Dài Yíng	代 (Dài): Take the place of	迎 (Yíng): Welcome; Greet
876	Huan Pei Dongfang	东方欢培	Dōngfāng Huān Péi	欢 (Huān): Joyous; merry; Jubilant;	培 (Péi): Training;

				vigorously	cultivate; Earth up; foster
877	Ying Ling Baili	百里盈令	Bǎilǐ Yíng Lìng	盈 (Yíng): Be full of; Be filled with	令 (Lìng): Order; command; decree
878	Xiao Yue Ximen	西门肖悦	Xīmén Xiào Yuè	肖 (Xiào): Resemble; Be like	悦 (Yuè): Happy; Pleased
879	Huan Juan Gongsun	公孙环娟	Gōngsūn Huán Juān	环 (Huán): Ring; hoop; link; Surround;	娟 (Juān): Graceful; Beautiful
880	Zhi Yin Gongliang	公良芝崟	Gōngliáng Zhī Yín	芝 (Zhī): A surname; Glossy ganoderma	崟 (Yín): High and steep;
881	Xi Liu Yuwen	宇文溪六	Yǔwén Xī Liù	溪 (Xī): Stream; Brook; rivulet	六 (Liù): Six; 6; number six
882	Jing Han Llvqu	闾丘京寒	Lǘqiū Jīng Hán	京 (Jīng): The capital of a country; Short for Beijing	寒 (Hán): Cold; Afraid; fearful
883	Yue Xi Chanyu	单于悦喜	Chányú Yuè Xǐ	悦 (Yuè): Happy; Pleased	喜 (Xǐ): Be happy; be delighted; Be pleased; be fond of
884	Xuan Ya Yuezheng	乐正旋娅	Yuèzhèng Xuán Yà	旋 (Xuán): Revolve; circle; spin; return; Soon	娅 (Yà): Ya, used in name; Husbands of sisters
885	Yu Yu Zhangsun	长孙瑜昱	Zhǎngsūn Yú Yù	瑜 (Yú): Yoga; Fine jade; gem	昱 (Yù): Sunlight; Sunshine
886	Pei Yan Gongyang	公羊培燕	Gōngyáng Péi Yàn	培 (Péi): Training; cultivate; Earth up; foster	燕 (Yàn): Swallow; Feast
887	Yin Lu Sikou	司寇寅露	Sīkòu Yín Lù	寅 (Yín): Respectful; The third of the twelve Earthly Branches	露 (Lù): Dew; syrup; fruit juice
888	Zhen Jing Qidiao	漆雕真静	Qīdiāo Zhēn Jìng	真 (Zhēn): Genuine; Real	静 (Jìng): Still; Calm

889	Yan Lou Zhuansun	颛孙艳露	Zhuānsūn Yàn Lòu	艳 (Yàn): Gorgeous; colorful; Gaudy; amorous	露 (Lòu): Reveal; Show
890	Wu Hua Chunyu	淳于伍骅	Chúnyú Wǔ Huá	伍 (Wǔ): Five	骅 (Huá): Hualiu; Name of a famous horse
891	Yan Xuan Xianyu	鲜于艳璇	Xiānyú Yàn Xuán	艳 (Yàn): Gorgeous; colorful; Gaudy; amorous	璇 (Xuán): Fine jade;
892	Xin Juan Xuanyuan	轩辕昕娟	Xuānyuán Xīn Juān	昕 (Xīn): Day; Sunrise	娟 (Juān): Graceful; Beautiful
893	Fang Yue Sima	司马放月	Sīmǎ Fàng Yuè	放 (Fàng): Release; Set free	月 (Yuè): Moon; Month
894	Yi Jing Nangong	南宫怡泾	Nángōng Yí Jīng	怡 (Yí): Happy; Joyful	泾 (Jīng): Short for the Jinghe River;
895	Yu Man Zhongli	钟离蔚曼	Zhōnglí Yù Màn	蔚 (Yù): A surname;	曼 (Màn): Graceful; Soft and beautiful
896	Ying Huan Diwu	第五莹欢	Dìwǔ Yíng Huān	莹 (Yíng): Jade-like stone; Lustrous and transparent	欢 (Huān): Joyous; merry; Jubilant; vigorously
897	Xue Shu Tuoba	拓跋雪淑	Tuòbá Xuě Shū	雪 (Xuě): Snow; Wipe out	淑 (Shū): Kind and gentle; Fair
898	Yan Jing Baili	百里颜静	Bǎilǐ Yán Jìng	颜 (Yán): Face; Countenance	静 (Jìng): Still; Calm
899	Zhu Duo Xuanyuan	轩辕珠朵	Xuānyuán Zhū Duǒ	珠 (Zhū): Bead; Pearl	朵 (Duǒ): Flower; A surname
900	Ya Wu Moqi	万俟雅吴	Mòqí Yǎ Wú	雅 (Yǎ): Refined; elegant; standard	吴 (Wú): Wu, a state in the Zhou Dynasty

901	Yue Wu Qiguan	亓官月伍	Qíguān Yuè Wǔ	月 (Yuè): Moon; Month	伍 (Wǔ): Five
902	Qiong Dong Yangshe	羊舌琼冬	Yángshé Qióng Dōng	琼 (Qióng): Fine jade;	冬 (Dōng): Winter; Rub-a-dub
903	Qing Hua Chunyu	淳于晴骅	Chúnyú Qíng Huá	晴 (Qíng): Clear; Fine	骅 (Huá): Hualiu; Name of a famous horse
904	Xi Qin Puyang	濮阳熙勤	Púyáng Xī Qín	熙 (Xī): Bright; sunny; prosperous	勤 (Qín): Diligent; industrious; Hardworking; often
905	Sha Wei Baili	百里沙蔚	Bǎilǐ Shā Wèi	沙 (Shā): Sand; granulated; powdered; Hoarse	蔚 (Wèi): Luxuriant; Grand
906	Ping Sha Tantai	澹台萍沙	Tántái Píng Shā	萍 (Píng): Duckweed;	沙 (Shā): Sand; granulated; powdered; Hoarse
907	Yu Yi Dongfang	东方语薏	Dōngfāng Yù Yì	语 (Yù): Tell; Inform	薏 (Yì): The heart of a lotus seed; Jobs tears
908	Ying Yi Gongye	公冶迎依	Gōngyě Yíng Yī	迎 (Yíng): Welcome; Greet	依 (Yī): Depend on; Rely on; comply with; listen to
909	Yue Wan Dongguo	东郭月曼	Dōngguō Yuè Wàn	月 (Yuè): Moon; Month	曼 (Wàn): A surname;
910	Yun Ze Situ	司徒昀则	Sītú Yún Zé	昀 (Yún): Sunlight; Sunshine	则 (Zé): Standard; norm; criterion
911	Qin Can Huyan	呼延勤灿	Hūyán Qín Càn	勤 (Qín): Diligent; industrious; Hardworking;	灿 (Càn): Bright; Illuminating

				often	
912	Song Wu Nanmen	南门宋伍	Nánmén Sòng Wǔ	宋 (Sòng): Song, a state in the Zhou Dynasty	伍 (Wǔ): Five
913	Xi Yue Gongliang	公良曦悦	Gōngliáng Xī Yuè	曦 (Xī): Sunlight (usually of early morning);	悦 (Yuè): Happy; Pleased
914	Xuan Qi Sikong	司空旋起	Sīkōng Xuán Qǐ	旋 (Xuán): Revolve; circle; spin; return; Soon	起 (Qǐ): Rise; get up; Stand up; draw out
915	Yi Yin Xiahou	夏侯艺崟	Xiàhóu Yì Yín	艺 (Yì): Art; Skill; norm; standard	崟 (Yín): High and steep;
916	Yang Xin Nanmen	南门扬昕	Nánmén Yáng Xīn	扬 (Yáng): Raise; throw up and scatter; Winnow; spread	昕 (Xīn): Day; Sunrise
917	Ting Duo Ziju	子车婷朵	Zǐjū Tíng Duǒ	婷 (Tíng): Graceful;	朵 (Duǒ): Flower; A surname
918	Ying Sha Dongmen	东门迎莎	Dōngmén Yíng Shā	迎 (Yíng): Welcome; Greet	莎 (Shā): Personal and place names
919	Ying Ying Tuoba	拓跋盈迎	Tuòbá Yíng Yíng	盈 (Yíng): Be full of; Be filled with	迎 (Yíng): Welcome; Greet
920	Qie Ya Gongsun	公孙伽丫	Gōngsūn Qié Yā	伽 (Qié): Temple; Samghrma	丫 (Yā): Ah; Bifurcation
921	Ying Hui Situ	司徒莹慧	Sītú Yíng Huì	莹 (Yíng): Jade-like stone; Lustrous and transparent	慧 (Huì): Wisdom; Intelligent
922	Wan Xing Qiguan	亓官婉幸	Qíguān Wǎn Xìng	婉 (Wǎn): Tactful; polite;	幸 (Xìng): Good fortune; favor

				Gracious; gentle and agreeable	
923	ga ga Zhuge	诸葛伽伽	Zhūgě gā gā	伽 (gā): Gamma;	伽 (gā): Gamma;
924	Xuan Nuan Dongfang	东方旋暖	Dōngfāng Xuàn Nuǎn	旋 (Xuàn): Whirl; turn something on a lathe	暖 (Nuǎn): Warm; Genial
925	Ying Feng Zhongsun	仲孙迎凤	Zhòngsūn Yíng Fèng	迎 (Yíng): Welcome; Greet	凤 (Fèng): Phoenix; A surname
926	Chun Hui Huyan	呼延淳惠	Hūyán Chún Huì	淳 (Chún): Pure; Honest	惠 (Huì): Favor; kindness; benefit; Favor; give
927	Ling Yi Helian	赫连令依	Hèlián Líng Yī	令 (Líng): A surname;	依 (Yī): Depend on; Rely on; comply with; listen to
928	Nai Rui Murong	慕容耐瑞	Mùróng Nài Ruì	耐 (Nài): Be able to bear or endure; Tolerance	瑞 (Ruì): Auspicious; lucky
929	Bai Yue Zhangdu	仉督百玥	Zhǎngdū Bǎi Yuè	百 (Bǎi): Surname; Hundred	玥 (Yuè): A legendary supernatural pearl in ancient China;
930	Yu Yu Gongxi	公西语语	Gōngxī Yù Yù	语 (Yù): Tell; Inform	语 (Yù): Tell; Inform
931	Wan ga Helian	赫连曼伽	Hèlián Wàn gā	曼 (Wàn): A surname;	伽 (gā): Gamma;
932	Zhen Rui Taishu	太叔真瑞	Tàishū Zhēn Ruì	真 (Zhēn): Genuine; Real	瑞 (Ruì): Auspicious; lucky
933	Qin Zhen Sikong	司空琴真	Sīkōng Qín Zhēn	琴 (Qín): Qin, a seven-stringed plucked instrument	真 (Zhēn): Genuine; Real
934	Meng Mei	闾丘梦梅	Lǘqiū	梦 (Mèng):	梅 (Méi): Plum;

			Llvqu		Mèng Méi	Dream;	Prunus mume

935	Xia Feng Linghu	令狐霞凤	Lìnghú Xiá Fèng	霞 (Xiá): Rosy clouds; Morning or evening glow	凤 (Fèng): Phoenix; A surname
936	Ting Wei Yuezheng	乐正婷蔚	Yuèzhèng Tíng Wèi	婷 (Tíng): Graceful;	蔚 (Wèi): Luxuriant; Grand
937	Yan Xiao Tantai	澹台颜肖	Tántái Yán Xiāo	颜 (Yán): Face; Countenance	肖 (Xiāo): A surname;
938	Xi Jin Zhongli	钟离溪槿	Zhōnglí Xī Jǐn	溪 (Xī): Stream; Brook; rivulet	槿 (Jǐn): Hibiscus; Rose of Sharon
939	Tao Nai Gongxi	公西桃耐	Gōngxī Táo Nài	桃 (Táo): Peach; Peach-shaped things	耐 (Nài): Be able to bear; To endure
940	Yan Ying Zhuge	诸葛彦莹	Zhūgě Yàn Yíng	彦 (Yàn): Elegant; accomplished; A man of virtue and ability	莹 (Yíng): Jade-like stone; Lustrous and transparent
941	Xin Pei Zaifu	宰父新培	Zǎifù Xīn Péi	新 (Xīn): New; fresh; novel; up-to-date	培 (Péi): Training; cultivate; Earth up; foster
942	Dong Yu Liangqiu	梁丘冬语	Liángqiū Dōng Yù	冬 (Dōng): Winter; Rub-a-dub	语 (Yù): Tell; Inform
943	Nuo Ling Nanmen	南门娜令	Nánmén Nuó Lìng	娜 (Nuó): Fascinating elegant; Delicate and gentle	令 (Lìng): Order; command; decree
944	Sha Jin Diwu	第五沙槿	Dìwǔ Shā Jǐn	沙 (Shā): Sand; granulated; powdered; Hoarse	槿 (Jǐn): Hibiscus; Rose of Sharon
945	Yu Hua Xiahou	夏侯语骅	Xiàhóu Yǔ Huá	语 (Yǔ): Language; tongue; Words;	骅 (Huá): Hualiu; Name of a famous horse

				set phrase	
946	Yu Shi Sikou	司寇雨是	Sīkòu Yǔ Shì	雨 (Yǔ): Rain; Wet	是 (Shì): Yes; correct; right; true; Praise; justify
947	Yi Li Gongliang	公良怡丽	Gōngliáng Yí Lí	怡 (Yí): Happy; Joyful	丽 (Lí): Meet with;
948	Yi Sha Zuoqiu	左丘懿沙	Zuǒqiū Yì Shà	懿 (Yì): Exemplary; A virtuous woman	沙 (Shà): Shake;
949	Yue Yan Llvqu	闾丘月彦	Lǘqiū Yuè Yàn	月 (Yuè): Moon; Month	彦 (Yàn): A man of virtue and ability; A surname
950	Jing Jin Nangong	南宫靖槿	Nángōng Jìng Jǐn	靖 (Jìng): Peaceful; Tranquil	槿 (Jǐn): Hibiscus; Rose of Sharon
951	Na Zhao Murong	慕容娜昭	Mùróng Nà Zhāo	娜 (Nà): A word used in feminine names;	昭 (Zhāo): Show; Manifest
952	Juan Ping Gongyang	公羊娟萍	Gōngyáng Juān Píng	娟 (Juān): Graceful; Beautiful	萍 (Píng): Duckweed;
953	Tong Ying Sikong	司空童莹	Sīkōng Tóng Yíng	童 (Tóng): Child; young servant; Virgin	莹 (Yíng): Jade-like stone; Lustrous and transparent
954	Jin Juan Sikou	司寇槿娟	Sīkòu Jǐn Juān	槿 (Jǐn): Hibiscus; Rose of Sharon	娟 (Juān): Graceful; Beautiful
955	Ying Yi Helian	赫连滢仪	Hèlián Yíng Yí	滢 (Yíng): Crystal-clear;	仪 (Yí): Instrument; Meter; bearing
956	Tian Xian Zhuansun	颛孙甜娴	Zhuānsūn Tián Xián	甜 (Tián): Sweetness; Sweet; honeyed	娴 (Xián): Refined; Skilled
957	Xuan Jing Duanmu	端木旋泾	Duānmù Xuàn Jīng	旋 (Xuàn): Whirl; turn something on a	泾 (Jīng): Short for the Jinghe River;

				lathe	
958	Xun Ya Yuchi	尉迟勋丫	Yùchí Xūn Yā	勋 (Xūn): Merit; Meritorious service	丫 (Yā): Ah; Bifurcation
959	Xin Zhou Llvqu	闾丘昕周	Lǘqiū Xīn Zhōu	昕 (Xīn): Day; Sunrise	周 (Zhōu): Circumference; periphery; circuit; week
960	Rui Feng Sima	司马瑞凤	Sīmǎ Ruì Fèng	瑞 (Ruì): Auspicious; lucky	凤 (Fèng): Phoenix; A surname
961	Jing Dai Nangong	南宫靖代	Nángōng Jìng Dài	靖 (Jìng): Peaceful; Tranquil	代 (Dài): Take the place of
962	Tao Yuan Nanmen	南门桃媛	Nánmén Táo Yuàn	桃 (Táo): Peach; Peach-shaped things	媛 (Yuàn): Pretty girl; Beautiful women
963	Ping Yue Duangan	段干萍玥	Duàngān Píng Yuè	萍 (Píng): Duckweed;	玥 (Yuè): A legendary supernatural pearl in ancient China;
964	Ya Ling Xuanyuan	轩辕丫铃	Xuānyuán Yā Líng	丫 (Yā): Ah; Bifurcation	铃 (Líng): Bell; boll; Bud
965	Xuan Yue Xuanyuan	轩辕璇玥	Xuānyuán Xuán Yuè	璇 (Xuán): Fine jade;	玥 (Yuè): A legendary supernatural pearl in ancient China;
966	Yuan Chi Zhangdu	仉督媛驰	Zhǎngdū Yuàn Chí	媛 (Yuàn): Pretty girl; Beautiful women	驰 (Chí): Speed; Turn eagerly towards
967	Wei Xuan Chanyu	单于薇璇	Chányú Wēi Xuán	薇 (Wēi): Common vetch; Vicia sativa	璇 (Xuán): Fine jade;
968	Yi Si Diwu	第五意兕	Dìwǔ Yì Sì	意 (Yì): Meaning; idea;	兕 (Sì): Female rhinoceros;

				Wish; desire	
969	Yuan Si Duangan	段干媛兕	Duàngān Yuán Sì	媛 (Yuán): Pretty (used in female names);	兕 (Sì): Female rhinoceros;
970	ou Nai Duangan	段干欧耐	Duàngān Ōu Nài	欧 (Ōu): Short for Europe; A surname	耐 (Nài): Be able to bear or endure; Tolerance
971	Yun Xiang Zhangsun	长孙匀想	Zhǎngsūn Yún Xiǎng	匀 (Yún): Uniform; Even	想 (Xiǎng): Think; like; Guess; suppose; trust
972	Duo Zhuo Ziju	子车朵卓	Zǐjū Duǒ Zhuō	朵 (Duǒ): Flower; A surname	卓 (Zhuō): Table; Desk
973	Ling Zhou Wuma	巫马铃周	Wūmǎ Líng Zhōu	铃 (Líng): Bell; boll; Bud	周 (Zhōu): Circumference; periphery; circuit; week
974	Shu Zhi Zuoqiu	左丘淑芝	Zuǒqiū Shū Zhī	淑 (Shū): Kind and gentle; Fair	芝 (Zhī): A surname; Glossy ganoderma
975	Tian Ning Murong	慕容甜宁	Mùróng Tián Nìng	甜 (Tián): Sweetness; Sweet; honeyed	宁 (Nìng): Rather; Would rather
976	Chun Yi Zongzheng	宗政淳忆	Zōngzhèng Chún Yì	淳 (Chún): Pure; Honest	忆 (Yì): Recall; Recollect
977	Ya Su Yangshe	羊舌雅苏	Yángshé Yǎ Sū	雅 (Yǎ): Refined; elegant; standard	苏 (Sū): Revive; come to; Short for Suzhou; short for Jiangsu Province;
978	Xue Tan Yuchi	尉迟雪檀	Yùchí Xuě Tán	雪 (Xuě): Snow; Wipe out	檀 (Tán): Sandalwood;
979	ai Yu Liangqiu	梁丘爱瑜	Liángqiū Ài Yú	爱 (Ài): Love; like; Be fond of; be keen on	瑜 (Yú): Yoga; Fine jade; gem
980	Xin Sha Tuoba	拓跋新莎	Tuòbá Xīn Shā	新 (Xīn): New; fresh; novel; up-to-date	莎 (Shā): Personal and place names

981	Ling Yu Zhuge	诸葛灵雨	Zhūgě Líng Yǔ	灵 (Líng): Quick; clever; Bright; effective	雨 (Yǔ): Rain; Wet
982	Yi Feng Sikong	司空仪凤	Sīkōng Yí Fèng	仪 (Yí): Instrument; Meter; bearing	凤 (Fèng): Phoenix; A surname
983	Yang Yuan Duangan	段干扬媛	Duàngān Yáng Yuàn	扬 (Yáng): Raise; throw up and scatter; Winnow; spread	媛 (Yuàn): Pretty girl; Beautiful women
984	Nuo Yang Rangsi	壤驷诺扬	Rǎngsì Nuò Yáng	诺 (Nuò): Promise; Yes	扬 (Yáng): Raise; throw up and scatter; Winnow; spread
985	Yuan Yin Puyang	濮阳媛胤	Púyáng Yuán Yìn	媛 (Yuán): Pretty (used in female names);	胤 (Yìn): Offspring; Posterity
986	Yi Yan Yuezheng	乐正仪燕	Yuèzhèng Yí Yān	仪 (Yí): Instrument; Meter; bearing	燕 (Yān): A surname; North Hebei
987	Nai Fang Nangong	南宫耐放	Nángōng Nài Fàng	耐 (Nài): Be able to bear; To endure	放 (Fàng): Release; Set free
988	Ning Ruo Huyan	呼延宁若	Hūyán Nìng Ruò	宁 (Nìng): Rather; Would rather	若 (Ruò): Like; seem; As if
989	Man Shu Zhuge	诸葛曼淑	Zhūgě Màn Shū	曼 (Màn): Graceful; Soft and beautiful	淑 (Shū): Kind and gentle; Fair
990	Nai Xiang Sikong	司空奈想	Sīkōng Nài Xiǎng	奈 (Nài): But; however; Tackle; deal with; bear stand	想 (Xiǎng): Think; like; Guess; suppose; trust
991	Xin Tan Gongliang	公良心檀	Gōngliáng Xīn Tán	心 (Xīn): The heart; Mind	檀 (Tán): Sandalwood;

992	Fen Xuan Tantai	澹台芬璇	Tántái Fēn Xuán	芬 (Fēn): Sweet smell; Fragrance	璇 (Xuán): Fine jade;
993	Yi Xuan Duangan	段干仪璇	Duàngān Yí Xuán	仪 (Yí): Instrument; Meter; bearing	璇 (Xuán): Fine jade;
994	Lou Ya Zhuge	诸葛露雅	Zhūgě Lòu Yǎ	露 (Lòu): Reveal; Show	雅 (Yǎ): Refined; elegant; standard
995	Jin Xin Zhuansun	颛孙槿心	Zhuānsūn Jǐn Xīn	槿 (Jǐn): Hibiscus; Rose of Sharon	心 (Xīn): The heart; Mind
996	Yi Zhuo Nanmen	南门依卓	Nánmén Yī Zhuō	依 (Yī): Depend on; Rely on; comply with; listen to	卓 (Zhuō): Table; Desk
997	Hui Nuo Duanmu	端木慧娜	Duānmù Huì Nuó	慧 (Huì): Wisdom; Intelligent	娜 (Nuó): Fascinating elegant; Delicate and gentle
998	Tan Wan Diwu	第五檀婉	Dìwǔ Tán Wǎn	檀 (Tán): Sandalwood;	婉 (Wǎn): Tactful; polite; Gracious; gentle and agreeable
999	Fang Qie Yuezheng	乐正方伽	Yuèzhèng Fāng Qié	方 (Fāng): Square; involution	伽 (Qié): Temple; Samghrma
1000	Nai Li Yuwen	宇文耐莉	Yǔwén Nài Lì	耐 (Nài): Be able to bear; To endure	莉 (Lì): Jasmine; Jasmine flower

Milton Keynes UK
Ingram Content Group UK Ltd.
UKHW032049040823
426331UK00012B/447

9 798889 191254